THE BEST OF THE BEST

THE BEST
OF THE BEST

Recipes from America's top restaurants,
famous chefs, and good cooks I've known

Arthur Hettich
Foreword by Jean Hewitt

Times BOOKS

Third printing, July 1979

Many of the recipes in this book originally appeared in *Family Circle*.

Book design: Beth Tondreau

Library of Congress Cataloging in Publication Data

Main entry under title:

The Best of the best.

   1. Cookery.   I. Hettich, Arthur, 1927–
TX652.B476   641.5   76–9715
ISBN 0–8129–0644–6

Contents

Foreword

I cannot think of anyone better qualified to offer a highly selective, Best of the Best collection of recipes than Arthur Hettich. His years of tasting thousands of dishes from chefs, food writers, good cooks and cookbooks in order to choose the best for *Family Circle*, and his constant search for the greatest food—from the finest restaurants in New York, around the U.S.A. and on frequent travels abroad—have given him the authority to choose the BEST.

Arthur Hettich knows that the Four Seasons Grill Room steak tartare varies little from the Carpaccio served at Harry's Bar in Florence and that Helen McCully's Own Special Quiche is tops. And if you've ever been faced with a shelf full of cookbooks when planning a menu, or choosing a dish for a special occasion, you'll appreciate that this book has done the sifting and selecting for you. Each of the Best of the Best recipes is a winner in flavor and appearance and, just as important, they can all be made by anyone in a modestly equipped kitchen because the directions are clear and no step, or ingredient, is missing. This clarity was one important criterion Arthur Hettich considered in writing the book because, as a weekend chef, he wanted to prepare all the dishes with no difficulty and get first-rate results.

A Best of the Best Dinner might start with a superb, no-bake pâté from Louis Szathmary's Bakery restaurant in Chicago, followed by Roger Chauveron's unusual pale green vichyssoise. Choosing from among the fifty-six main dishes that range from Myra Waldo's hamburgers to Sheryl Julian's Gougère with mushrooms and ham, and include Mexican, Chinese, Italian and Japanese specialties, takes a little more thought. How about roast fresh ham from the barbecue with apple sauce, or baked in the oven and served with Cumberland sauce and accompanied by Arthur's own home fries? From among the eight great salads I'd pick Peg Bracken's sour cream cole slaw.

You could set out an international display of Best of the Best desserts

and include Ernie's of San Francisco French Apple Tart, Fauchon's
wildly rich chocolate mousse, Nika Hazelton's Rødgrød and Arthur's
mother's mocha nut butter cookies. And what could be better than
Burt Reynolds' Parmesan Garlic toast when you're hungry for a snack?
Whatever you choose to cook from the book, I guarantee you'll enjoy
The Best of the Best.

Jean D. Hewitt

Preface

Over the past several years, as editor of *Family Circle*, I've had the enjoyable task of tasting thousands of recipes, many of them created by top food writers, four-star restaurant chefs, famous gourmets, and some of the fine grass-roots cooks located in every section of the country.

The recipes in this book are "the best" of these best—my own personal favorites selected from the countless numbers of good dishes I've tasted, and the best I was able to find for popular dishes ranging from apple pie to steak tartare. I tried dozens of cheesecakes, for example, before finally judging John Clancy's as the best, and consumed numerous helpings of chili, recipes for which came from all over the country, before finding the consummate spoonful right in my own backyard—from Craig Claiborne, of all people.

The selections range from the simplest dishes, like Mimi Sheraton's hot dogs, through more specialized but still easy-to-make fare like the *carpaccio* I discovered in Harry's Bar in Florence, to a cassoulet by Perla Meyers, which certainly does require time and effort but is well worth every minute—and is most fun, perhaps, if you turn it into a group effort for a rainy weekend, as I've done at home.

All the recipes have been tested for accuracy and clarity so that anyone can easily follow them. To be perfectly honest, I'm a terrible cook when left on my own. But when I use the recipes in this book, I become a veritable "great chef."

Restaurant chefs, incidentally, are a marvelous source for good recipes, but they often seem unable to put down on paper what they actually do. This problem was solved by having professional home economists work directly with my favorite restaurant chefs to get their recipes straight and gear them to family-size servings.

This book has been a labor of love all the way, partly because of the attractive subject matter and because working on it brought me in contact with many talented and interesting people. I want to thank them all here for their sparkling contributions:

Nancy Fitzpatrick helped me with every phase of editorial preparation. Nancy is a terrific editor and a good friend.

Marie Walsh straightened out the sometimes garbled recipes I brought back from restaurants or friends. She also gave me a great recipe of her own.

Jean Hewitt always seemed to know where to go for "the best." She also provided her warm support—and the foreword to this book.

Jane O'Keefe gave me the benefit of her vast food expertise and also a great recipe for apple pie.

Eleanore Lewis helped me keep organized and if you've ever seen my desk, you'll know that's no mean feat.

Anna Marie Doherty and Linda Dannenberg helped find some really wonderful recipes. So did Curt Anderson, Jean Anderson, Susanna and Jason Berger, Joan Hirschman, Barbara Kraus, Robert Lescher, Grace Manney, Patricia Myrer, and James Trager.

Last but far from least, I want to thank all of the fine creative food experts who contributed the marvelous recipes that follow.

THE BEST OF THE BEST

Best of the Best Appetizers

The Bakery's No-Bake Pâté Maison
Eli's Chopped Liver
Oysters Kilpatrick
Shrimp Sakowitz
Dora Jonassen's Marinated Salmon with
   Mustard-Dill Sauce
Marie Walsh's Ham-Stuffed Mushrooms
Poor Man's Caviar
Indonesian Satés with Pepper Relish
Helen Feingold's Barbecued Chicken Drumettes
Helen McCully's Own Special Quiche
Peg Bracken's "Best and Easiest" Canapé
Smoked Salmon Spread in Pumpernickel
Nika Hazelton's Marinated Green or
   Red Sweet Peppers
Nika's Blender Cheddar-Beer Dip

The Bakery's No-Bake Pâté Maison

Until I discovered the pâté served at the Bakery Restaurant in Chicago, I always had shied away from making this popular appetizer at home. I love pâté, but most recipes involve molding or shaping a mixture of meats and seasonings into a pastry crust or terrine mold which is then baked and sealed with aspic. All this takes time—and more patience than I have. But the Bakery's chef, Louis Szathmary, makes a pâté that eliminates all these steps. Chef Louis, who is also author of The Chef's Secret Cook Book, *likes the recipe so much himself that it's the one item on his "unprinted" menu he serves every day.*

In using the recipe you'll notice that one of the ingredients, pâté spice, actually has a separate recipe. This blending of herbs and spices can be made ahead of time and stored in a tightly covered jar to use whenever you make the pâté, or as a seasoning ingredient with other foods including beef pot roast, meat loaf, lamb and veal ragouts, or roasted meats. I think you'll enjoy the spice blend, and I know you'll find the pâté irresistible.

Makes about 16 servings

1 large onion, minced (1 cup)
¾ cup lard, or chicken or duck fat (no other shortening will do)
½ pound chicken or duck livers
2 cups (about ¾ pound) cooked meat (any roasted, broiled, boiled, baked, braised, or fried meat, especially chicken with skin, duck, turkey, pork, veal, beef, or a combination, but not lamb or mutton)
6 tablespoons unsalted butter at room temperature
2–3 tablespoons brandy or cognac
2 teaspoons Pâté Spice (recipe follows)

1. Sauté onion in ½ cup lard until very soft, but not brown. Add livers, raise heat, and cook until the last traces of pink disappear. Cool.
2. Grind the cooked meat three times, using the medium-size holes in the meat grinder. Then grind the livers and onion together three times.
3. Beat butter and remaining lard together in electric mixer; blend in ground liver and meat, beating at low speed until fluffy. Mix in brandy and pâté spice.
4. Taste; add more salt or pâté spice if necessary. Chill. Serve as an appetizer with pickles and crusty bread.

Note: In this recipe the method is really more important than the ingredients. You have a choice of using lard, chicken fat (schmaltz), or duck fat. You can use chicken livers or duck livers or a mixture of the two. Several different kinds of cooked meat can be used, but do not try to change the procedure or combine the steps.

Note that in steps 1 and 3 you *must* use lard or chicken or duck fat. Most any natural shortening will give the pâté its necessary fluffiness. Oil will *not* work, and man-made shortening will give the pâté a taste of tallow.

The amount of brandy or cognac can be adjusted somewhat, but if you do not wish to use alcohol in the pâté, you should add 2 or 3 tablespoons of some other liquid, such as chicken or beef broth, for proper consistency.

Pâté Spice

Makes ¼ cup

HERBS

1½ teaspoons very finely crushed bay leaf
1½ teaspoons very finely crushed thyme
1½ teaspoons very finely crushed rosemary
1½ teaspoons very finely crushed basil

SPICES

2½ teaspoons ground cinnamon
1½ teaspoons ground mace
¾ teaspoon ground cloves
¼ teaspoon ground allspice
½ teaspoon ground white pepper
1 teaspoon Spanish or Hungarian paprika
¼ cup salt

1. Crush the herbs together in a spice mortar or in a deep bowl with the bottom of a cup.
2. Sift the herbs through a fine sieve two or three times, crushing again whatever remains in the sieve, until everything is sifted.
3. Mix herbs with spices and salt; store in a tightly closed jar.

Eli's Chopped Liver

Eli Schulman, the gruff-voiced good-humored owner of "Eli's, The Place for Steaks" in Chicago, makes a point of getting to know everyone who comes into his restaurant. Eli also makes sure that everyone tastes the restaurant's well-known chopped liver appetizer. It's served like caviar, with minced onion and chopped hard-boiled eggs, and Eli reports that his clients—a lively, sophisticated crowd of diners from the world of sports, theater, government, and business—like it better than caviar. Give it a try.

Makes about 3 cups

1 pound chicken livers
2 medium onions, chopped
⅓ cup rendered chicken fat
2 hard-boiled eggs
1 teaspoon salt
½ teaspoon pepper

1. Sauté livers and onions in chicken fat in a large skillet until no pink remains in livers and onions are golden brown.
2. Chop livers, onions, and eggs coarsely and evenly, or, put through food grinder using coarsest blade. Do not use electric blender. Stir in salt and pepper gently. Refrigerate.
3. Serve garnished with additional chopped egg and parsley sprigs,

if you wish. It may also be served in scoops on lettuce leaves, garnished with minced onion and chopped egg. Or, it may be spread on crisp, thin crackers or toast, or used to stuff celery.

Oysters Kilpatrick

On a recent trek to Australia, I discovered an oyster dish that I consider the most delicious I've ever tasted. (Of course, unadulterated oysters on the half-shell are pretty terrific to begin with.) Similar to clams casino, Oysters Kilpatrick are, in fact, so popular that they're served in practically every Australian restaurant, and in many homes such as that of Ann and John Southam of North Turramurra. John is the publisher of Family Circle's Australian edition and while visiting the Southams, I was able to convince Ann to give me the recipe. I'm glad I did—and I think you will be too.

Makes 2 servings

1 dozen oysters in their shells
Rock salt
Worcestershire sauce
Salt
Pepper
4 slices bacon, diced and fried
Chopped parsley

1. Open oysters. Make a layer of rock salt in the bottom of a baking dish; place oysters on rock salt. Season oysters to taste with a drop or two of worcestershire sauce, salt, and pepper and sprinkle with the cooked bacon.
2. Broil, 4 inches from the heat, for 3 minutes, or just until the oysters begin to curl. Sprinkle with parsley and serve.

Note: Clams may be substituted for the oysters.

Shrimp Sakowitz

The Sakowitz stores in Texas offer a wide range of international merchandise to residents of the state and to mail order customers around the country. They also offer a wonderful selection of foods, such as this shrimp appetizer, served in the stores' restaurants. When food writer Nika Hazelton reported on the foods of Texas for a recent issue of Family Circle, *she was able to obtain the recipe—and the method for serving the shrimp in a "tower" arrangement, which is particularly attractive on a buffet table.*

Makes 4 servings

1 **pound fresh shrimp**
2 **cups water**
3 **tablespoons lemon juice**
1 **tablespoon salt**
½ **teaspoon monosodium glutamate**
½ **teaspoon paprika**
  Red Cocktail Sauce Sakowitz (recipe follows)

1. Rinse shrimp in cold water; drain thoroughly.
2. Combine water, lemon juice, salt, monosodium glutamate, and paprika in large saucepan. Heat to boiling; drop in shrimp. Cover tightly; simmer for 5 minutes, or until shrimp are pink.
3. Drain shrimp; cover with cold water. Drain again, peel, and de-vein. Rinse each shrimp in cold water. Drain on paper toweling.
4. Refrigerate shrimp until serving time. Serve with Red Cocktail Sauce Sakowitz.

Red Cocktail Sauce Sakowitz

Makes 1½ cups

¾ cup ketchup
½ cup chili sauce
1 tablespoon horseradish
2 teaspoons lemon juice
½ teaspoon worcestershire sauce
½ green pepper, seeded and finely chopped
1 teaspoon finely chopped celery

1. Combine all ingredients; mix well. Chill in refrigerator at least 1 hour.
2. Serve with Shrimp Sakowitz.

Shrimp Tower

To make a shrimp tower fasten parsley sprigs in a spiral design on Styrofoam cone (available in variety and hardware stores), using toothpicks broken in half. Leave 1 to 2 inches between spirals for cooked Shrimp Sakowitz. Fasten the shrimp with whole toothpicks so that they may be pulled out for eating.

Dora Jonassen's Marinated Salmon with Mustard-Dill Sauce

It takes an especially talented person like Dora Jonassen to prepare food that can stand up to a camera's scrutinizing eye. But Dora does much more than just prepare food. She also develops recipes and works side-by-side with the photographer to make sure the pictures you see in a magazine are what they should be. This is why her work is always in demand at Family Circle *and at most other women's magazines. After spending a day in the kitchen and under a photographer's lights, Dora doesn't feel much like cooking at home. But she does enjoy it when the pressure is off, and this recipe is one of her favorites. "I always serve* gravlaks *(marinated salmon) at Christmas time as an appetizer," says Dora, "and in summer it's nice for lunch with ice cold aquavit and beer." After having tried this Danish specialty myself, I think it should be served year round. See if you don't agree.*

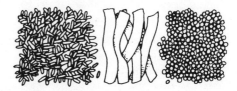

Makes about 12 servings as an appetizer, or 6 to 8 servings as a light luncheon dish

2½–3 pounds fresh salmon
 ⅓ cup coarse salt
 2 tablespoons sugar
 1 teaspoon crushed white peppercorns
 6 whole allspice, crushed
 1 bunch fresh dill
   Mustard-Dill Sauce (recipe follows)

1. If possible, select a middle or center cut from salmon. Scale and bone the fish (or have the fish market do it for you). Combine salt, sugar, peppercorns, and allspice. Sprinkle over salmon and rub slightly into surface.
2. Place a few sprigs of dill in a shallow glass bowl or baking dish. Place one half of salmon, skin-side down, on dill; cover with plenty of dill. Place remaining salmon, skin-side up, on top; add a few more sprigs of dill. Cover with plastic wrap.
3. Place a plate on top of fish; weigh down with a 2-pound can or weight. Refrigerate for 48 hours, turning salmon every 12 hours. (This will keep up to 1 week in refrigerator.)
4. When ready to serve, scrape off spices and dill; place salmon skin-side down on cutting board. Slice across grain into thin slices, detaching each slice from the skin. Arrange slices on serving plate garnished with fresh dill and lemon slices. Serve with mustard-dill sauce and dark bread.

Mustard-Dill Sauce

Makes 1 cup

⅓ cup prepared brown mustard
 2 tablespoons sugar
1–2 teaspoons dry mustard
 2 tablespoons vinegar
 ½ cup salad oil
 ¼ cup chopped fresh dill

1. Combine prepared mustard, sugar, dry mustard, and vinegar in small bowl. Add oil in a thin stream, while beating constantly with a wire whisk.
2. Stir in dill. Cover; refrigerate several hours for flavors to blend.

Marie Walsh's Ham-Stuffed Mushrooms

When Marie Walsh, editor of many Family Circle cookbooks, invited some of her peers for cocktails recently, she was a bit apprehensive. Food people can be very critical, you know. Well, Marie needn't have worried. Her hors d'oeuvres were great—especially these stuffed mushrooms. Extra added attraction: Most of the work can be done a day or two in advance. In fact, Marie notes, the flavor is even better if the preparation is done ahead of time.

Makes 24 large mushrooms

2 pounds large mushrooms
8 tablespoons (1 stick) butter
1 package (4 ounces) Danish sliced ham, diced
2 cups Freshly Toasted White Bread Crumbs (recipe follows)
½ cup chopped parsley
¼ cup dry vermouth

1. Wipe mushrooms with a damp cloth; remove stems and save for the soup pot.
2. Melt half the butter in a large skillet over low heat. Arrange a layer of mushroom caps in pan and sauté for 3 minutes; turn and sauté for 3 minutes on second side. Arrange cooked mushrooms in a jelly-roll pan. Continue until all caps are sautéed, adding more butter, if needed.
3. Add remaining butter to skillet; sauté ham for 5 minutes. Stir in toasted bread crumbs, parsley, and dry vermouth until well-blended; remove from the heat. Divide mixture among mushroom caps, pressing into a rounded mound on top to fill generously. Cover pan with aluminum foil. Refrigerate until serving time.
4. Bake in moderate oven, 350 degrees, for 15 minutes, or until piping hot. Serve on heated plates.

Note: Actually, these mushrooms are just as good cold, but hot hors d'oeuvres should be served hot. Any leftover caps can be served chilled the next night.

Freshly Toasted White Bread Crumbs

Makes 4 cups

Break 4 slices white bread into quarters and place 4 quarters at a time into an electric blender. Cover blender, process on high just until crumbs are formed, then spread on a jelly-roll pan. Continue until all slices are crumbed. Bake in a slow oven, 325 degrees, for 15 minutes, or until golden-brown, stirring several times while baking.

Poor Man's Caviar

Joan Hirschman is a successful young painter—and a marvelous cook. Her canvases have brought her numerous gallery showings and much recognition in New York art circles; her cooking has brought her rave reviews from family and friends.

With a demanding career, Joan usually has less time for cooking than she might like, but during her summers in Europe she catches up on this second love by collecting some of the local food specialties throughout the countries she visits.

This recipe, called tapenade, *is one she found on a recent trip to France. It's a Provençal version of caviar— but a lot cheaper than caviar. It's also a pungent mixture that only gets better with time, making it the ideal make-ahead hors d'oeuvre. Of course, you can serve it right away but it is best after it has been stashed in the refrigerator for a day or two.*

Serve it on buttered (unsalted) toast or use it to stuff scooped-out cherry tomatoes or hard-boiled eggs. Anyway you serve it, it's going to bring you compliments as an artist in your own right.

Makes about 20 hors d'oeuvres

4 ounces Greek olives (pitted) or 6 ounces ripe California olives, pitted and drained
1 2-ounce can flat anchovies, rinsed well with cold water and dried
2 tablespoons capers, drained
¼ cup olive oil
1 teaspoon leaf thyme (use 1½ teaspoons if using California olives)
¼ teaspoon dry mustard (½ teaspoon with California olives)
1 tablespoon cognac (optional)

1. Put all the ingredients in an electric blender. Grind to a coarse paste.
2. Serve immediately, or let the flavors blend for a day or two in the refrigerator.

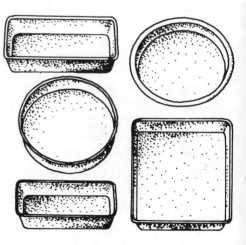

Indonesian Satés with Pepper Relish

Over the years, home economics consultant Helen Feingold has worked with dozens of magazines, newspapers, food companies, ad agencies, and cookbook writers in developing, testing, and photographing hundreds of foods. This is one recipe she created for Family Circle *—along with the barbecued chicken drumettes which follows; and they're both show stoppers. If she keeps this up, Helen will be writing her own cookbook before long. I can't think of anyone better qualified for the job.*

Makes 27 small skewers

¼ cup peanut oil
1 medium onion, chopped
2 cloves garlic, minced
1 tomato, peeled and chopped
2 tablespoons peanut butter
1 13¾-ounce can chicken broth
1 6-ounce can tomato paste
½ teaspoon crushed red pepper
1 teaspoon salt
2 pounds skinless, boneless chicken breasts, cut into ½-inch cubes or 2 pounds lean, boneless pork, cut into ½-inch cubes
Pepper Relish (recipe follows)

1. In a large skillet, heat oil and sauté onion, garlic, and tomato until very thick. Stir in peanut butter, chicken broth, and tomato paste. Add red pepper. Simmer, stirring constantly for 5 minutes. Add salt. Cool.
2. Spear 2 cubes of chicken or pork on each heatproof skewer. Place skewers side by side in a shallow glass pan. Spoon sauce over meat and let stand, covered, in refrigerator until ready to serve.
3. Place under broiler and broil for 5 to 6 minutes on each side, or until chicken is lightly browned and hot, or until pork pieces are thoroughly cooked. Serve very hot with pepper relish spooned over each skewer.

Pepper Relish

Makes 1⅔ cups

8 ounces sweet pickled red and green cherry peppers
1 4-ounce jar pimiento, drained
½ navel orange, peeled and cubed
½ cup chopped celery
1 teaspoon sugar

1. Halve cherry peppers and remove seeds and stems. Place peppers and remaining ingredients into an electric blender and whirl at medium speed until finely chopped.
2. Chill until ready to serve. Serve with Indonesian Satés.

Helen Feingold's Barbecued Chicken Drumettes

Makes about 8 servings

  3 pounds chicken wings
  ½ teaspoon salt
  ¼ teaspoon pepper
  ¼ cup vegetable oil
  1 Bermuda onion, chopped
  2 cloves garlic, chopped
  1 cup ketchup
  ½ cup apricot preserves
  1 tablespoon worcestershire sauce
  ¼ teaspoon Tabasco

1. Remove tips on each chicken wing and cut remaining wing into 2 pieces at the joint. Place pieces side-by-side in a shallow glass dish and sprinkle with salt and pepper.
2. Heat oil in a large skillet and sauté onion and garlic until golden, about 5 minutes. Stir in ketchup, preserves, worcestershire sauce, and Tabasco; simmer for 5 minutes. Cool and then pour evenly over chicken wings. Chill for several hours or overnight.
3. When ready to serve, place wings in a single layer in a shallow baking pan. Bake in a moderate oven, 350 degrees, for 40 minutes, or until wings are tender. Serve hot.

Helen McCully's Own Special Quiche

Nobody Ever Tells You These Things is one of Helen McCully's best-selling books. It's also something I learned when I made quiche for the first time; no one had ever mentioned how simple it is, particularly when you have one of Helen's recipes to work with.

This version of quiche sticks to the nitty gritty of the idea, avoiding excessive steps or ingredients but never sacrificing on the final results. And I think it's this imaginative but down-to-earth approach to food that has helped make Helen so successful as a cookbook author and as food editor for House Beautiful.

Makes 1 9-inch quiche

  1 partially baked 9-inch pastry shell
  6–8 slices bacon
  3 eggs
  2 cups heavy cream
    Salt
    Pepper
    Freshly ground nutmeg

1. Prepare your favorite single-crust piecrust recipe and bake in a quiche pan in a hot oven, 425 degrees, for 10 minutes. Remove from oven and lower oven temperature to moderate, 350 degrees.

2. While crust is baking, cook bacon until brown. Drain and crumble it. Scatter bacon bits over bottom of pastry shell; set aside.

3. Beat eggs and cream together lightly; stir in salt, pepper, and nutmeg to taste. Pour over the bacon.

4. Place filled quiche pan on a baking sheet (to catch any spills), and bake in moderate oven, 350 degrees, for 25 minutes, or until a paring knife inserted 1 inch from the center comes out clean.

5. Serve immediately, piping hot, as an hors d'oeuvre; or as an entrée for lunch or a light supper, with green salad vinaigrette, French bread, and a chilled white wine.

"It's not exotic at all," notes Peg, "but every single one is always eaten, which is more than you can say for most canapés."

White bread, thinly sliced
Mayonnaise
Parmesan cheese
Onion, thinly sliced

1. Cut small circles from bread using a small biscuit cutter. Spread them with mayonnaise and then sprinkle them lavishly with parmesan cheese.

2. On each one, put a thin slice of onion, preferably just a little smaller than the bread round.

3. Just before serving, toast under the broiler until bubbly and very hot, and the onions are just slightly brown.

Peg Bracken's "Best and Easiest" Canapé

Peg Bracken is internationally known for her witty newspaper and magazine columns as well as for the best-selling I Hate to Cook Book. *But for someone who professes not to like cooking, Peg always comes through with winning recipes like this one.*

Smoked Salmon Spread in Pumpernickel

Here's one way you can avoid k.p. after a party. The appetizer is a tangy spread that fits right into its own edible container—a loaf of pumpernickel bread.

Makes 2½ cups

- 1 unsliced round pumpernickel (approximately 1 pound)
- ½ pound smoked salmon
- 1 8-ounce package cream cheese
- ½ cup milk
- ⅓ cup chopped scallions
- 1 tablespoon lemon juice
  Drained capers

1. With a sharp knife, cut straight down into loaf of bread, cutting a circle in the center of the bread, leaving a narrow but sturdy ring of bread to use as the container for the spread. Cut the removed circle of bread into thin slices; wrap and chill. Wrap ring of bread.
2. Combine salmon, cream cheese, milk, scallions, and lemon juice in electric blender; whirl until smooth. Scrape into a bowl, cover, and chill.
3. When ready to serve, place ring of bread on a large platter. Fill center with salmon spread. Sprinkle with capers. Surround loaf with slices of bread; serve with a spreader.

Nika Hazelton's Marinated Green or Red Sweet Peppers

Nika Hazelton is a unique food writer in that she is respected and accepted by every level of the tightly structured food hierarchy—from our famous exponents of haute cuisine to the magazine home economist. That is because she knows good food wherever it originates—as do many of those home economists. These marinated peppers, for instance, may sound a bit tricky, but as you'll see from the directions, preparing them is really a matter of learning how to peel peppers and, as Nika says, "millions of Italian housewives do this daily, so there's no reason you can't." The peppers, by the way, are terrific on an antipasto tray.

1. Turn one burner on a gas range to medium high. Or heat a burner on an electric range to medium. Stand or lay several whole peppers on the burner so they will become charred. Turn them occasionally so that they

char evenly on all sides and the top and bottom as well.

2. As peppers are charred, lift them with tongs or a pot holder and place them under cold running water to cool. One at a time, holding peppers under cold running water, rub off charred parts. Drain peppers on paper toweling.

3. When all the peppers have been peeled, cut off tops. Then halve peppers and remove seeds and membranes. Wash peppers again, cut into strips, and drain well. Place in a shallow bowl and drizzle olive oil over them. Cover; store in the refrigerator to season for as long as three days.

Makes about 3 cups

1 8-ounce package cream cheese
¾ cup milk
¼ cup beer
2 cups (8 ounces) diced, sharp cheddar cheese
1 clove garlic, cut up
3 medium dill pickles, cut up

1. Combine cream cheese and milk in electric blender. Cover and beat at high speed for 10 seconds.

2. Add beer, cheddar cheese, and garlic. Cover and beat until smooth.

3. Add pickles; cover and blend for 3 seconds. Place in a serving bowl; chill. Serve with potato chips and corn chips.

Nika's Blender Cheddar-Beer Dip

Gourmets may turn up their noses at dips, but I like them; and this is a particular favorite of mine. Created by Nika Hazelton, it's a nice change from the inevitable onion dip, and it is a mixture that I can't stop eating once I get the crackers out.

Best of the Best Soups

Vichyssoise à la Roger Chauveron
Chilled Gazpacho from the Tack Room
Larry Kane's Chilled Soups
Bill Johnston's Manhattan Clam Chowder
Marcella Hazan's Minestrone
Brennan's Onion Soup au Gratin
Coach House Black Bean Soup
Danish Yellow Pea Soup

Vichyssoise à la Roger Chauveron

After years as the chef at New York's famed Café Chambord, and later owner–chef of Café Chauveron, Roger Chauveron retired to Florida. But the retirement was unsuccessful, and in a very short time he was back in the kitchen—this time at the new Café Chauveron in Bay Harbor, Florida. This vichyssoise is one of the fine specialties on his new menu, and it is worth trying there as well as at home.

Makes 6 servings

3 leeks (white part only), washed and thinly sliced
1 large onion, thinly sliced
⅛ pound (2 ounces) spinach or sorrel, washed and shredded
2 tablespoons unsalted butter
2 cans (13¾ ounces each) chicken broth (3 cups)
2 medium potatoes, peeled and diced
1 cup milk, scalded
½ teaspoon salt
Dash white pepper
½ cup heavy cream
Chopped chives

1. Sauté leek, onion, and spinach or sorrel slowly in butter in a large saucepan for 20 minutes, stirring occasionally. Vegetables should be soft, but not brown.

2. Stir in chicken broth and potatoes; cook 20 minutes longer or until potatoes are tender. Add milk; bring mixture to boiling; remove from heat.

3. Add salt and pepper. Taste; add more seasoning, if you wish. Puree soup through sieve or food mill, or in electric blender. Chill for several hours.

4. Stir cream into chilled soup. Serve in chilled cups with a sprinkling of chopped chives on each serving.

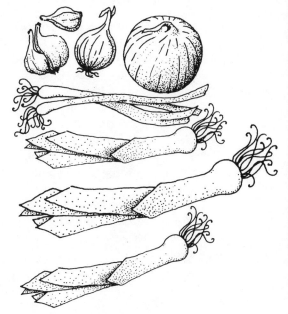

Chilled Gazpacho Soup from the Tack Room

The Tack Room Restaurant in Tucson, Arizona, has everything going for it. It is located in a Spanish-style hacienda on the banks of the Tanque Verde River overlooking the Sabino Canyon in the Santa Catalina Mountains. It's the perfect setting for scenic dining. But the menu here is superb, too, and includes this appetizer gazpacho. Served icy cold with plenty of croutons, it's unbeatable—with or without a view.

Makes about 6 servings

- 2 cans (14½ ounces each) sliced baby tomatoes
- 1 can (5¾ ounces drained weight) pitted black olives
- ¾ cup chopped celery
- ¾ cup chopped green onions
- ¾ cup chopped cucumber
- 2 cloves garlic, minced
- 3 tablespoons red wine vinegar
- 1½ tablespoons liquid seasoning for meats
- 1 teaspoon worcestershire sauce
- 6 drops Tabasco (or to taste)
- 1 10½-ounce can condensed beef broth
- ¾ cup dry white wine
- Chopped chives
- Croutons

1. Drain tomatoes over a large bowl. Cut tomato slices into large pieces; add to juice in bowl.
2. Drain olives; cut each into 3 slices. Add with celery, green onions, cucumber, and garlic to bowl. Stir in vinegar, liquid seasoning, worcestershire sauce, Tabasco, beef broth, and wine; cover. Chill for 24 hours.
3. To serve, ladle into chilled soup bowls. Garnish with chives and croutons.

Larry Kane's Chilled Soups

As associate editor at Family Circle, *Larry Kane has little to do with preparing food. But at home, things are different. He's an enthusiastic cook and so dedicated to perfection that if a recipe doesn't yield very special results, he keeps tinkering with it until it does. These soups are the results of some of his experimentation with two classics. They're thick and creamy and, in a word, perfect.*

Chilled Beet Soup

Makes 6 servings

4 tablespoons (½ stick) butter
1 large leek, chopped (¾ cup)
1 carrot, scraped and chopped (½ cup)
1 parsnip, pared and chopped (½ cup)
½ cup chopped celery
2 tablespoons chopped parsley
1 medium onion, chopped (½ cup)
2 cups chopped cooked beets (use fresh beets, not canned)
2 cans (10¼ ounces each) condensed beef broth
½ teaspoon salt
Pepper
¼ cup lemon juice
1 cup (½ pint) dairy sour cream

1. Melt butter in a large saucepan; sauté leek, carrot, parsnip, celery, parsley, and onion until almost tender. Add beets and broth; cover.
2. Bring to boiling; lower heat. Cover; simmer for 10 minutes. Remove from heat; cool slightly.
3. Pour part of the soup into an electric blender; cover. Whirl until smooth. (Or puree through sieve or food mill.) Pour into a large bowl. Repeat until all the soup is pureed. Stir in salt. Add pepper to taste and lemon juice. Chill at least 4 hours.
4. Pour into chilled serving bowls.

Garnish with sour cream. Sprinkle with chopped chives, if you wish. Serve icy cold.

Chilled Watercress Soup

Makes 6 servings

1 large bunch watercress
6 tablespoons (¾ stick) butter
4 large leeks, chopped (2 cups)
3 tablespoons flour
3 envelopes (3 teaspoons) instant chicken broth
1 teaspoon salt
1 teaspoon leaf basil, crumbled
3 cups water
2 cups plain yogurt

1. Wash and pick over watercress. Remove stems and measure leaves. (You should have 2 cups.)
2. Melt butter in a large, heavy saucepan. Sauté leeks and watercress just until wilted, but do not allow to brown.
3. Stir in flour, instant chicken broth, salt, and basil. Cook, stirring constantly, until mixture bubbles (about 1 minute); stir in water. Heat slowly to boiling; lower heat. Cover; simmer for 15 minutes. Remove saucepan from heat; cool.
4. Pour part of the soup into an electric blender; cover. Whirl until smooth. Repeat until all soup is pureed.

5. Pour into a large bowl. Stir in yogurt. Cover; chill at least 4 hours.
6. Pour into chilled serving bowls. Garnish with sprigs of watercress and slices of radish, if you wish. Serve icy cold.

Bill Johnston's Manhattan Clam Chowder

Bill Johnston says that the secret of making good clam chowder is to have lots of freshly shucked clams, to chop and cook them for only two minutes in a vegetable/clam broth mixture, and to use no salt and little or no water so the full fragrance of the clams predominates.

The secret for me is to use Bill's recipe, one which has earned him a reputation as a good cook among his family and friends in East Hampton, Long Island.

During his years as executive director of the Board of Trade of the Wholesale Sea Food Merchants, Inc., Bill was only able to spend weekends in this beautiful beach community. But since his retirement not long ago, he now spends all his time there and actively pursues his cooking—and his digging for all those fresh clams.

Makes 6 servings

36 large chowder clams (quahogs) or 2 cans (7–8 ounces each) minced clams
4 tablespoons (½ stick) unsalted butter
1 large onion, diced (1 cup)
2 medium potatoes, diced (1½ cups)
1 cup diced celery
2 medium carrots, diced (¾ cup)
¼ cup diced green pepper
1 can (2 pounds, 3 ounces) Italian-style plum tomatoes, drained
1½ teaspoons leaf thyme, crumbled
¼ teaspoon white pepper
⅛ teaspoon curry powder

1. Shuck fresh clams; reserve broth. Chop clams coarsely. (If using canned clams, drain and reserve broth.) Broth from clams should measure 2 cups; if it does not, add water or bottled clam broth.
2. Melt butter in a large saucepan. Sauté onions until lightly browned.
3. Add remaining ingredients and extra water, if needed, to cover vegetables. Bring to boil; lower heat. Cover and simmer for 30 minutes, or just until vegetables are tender.
4. Add fresh or canned clams. Turn off heat, cover, and let stand for 2 minutes, or just until clams are thoroughly hot. Serve with warm buttered pilot crackers, if you wish.

Marcella Hazan's Minestrone

This recipe is an authentic, un-Americanized version of one of Italy's renowned soups. It was given to me by Marcella Hazan, author of the Classic Italian Cookbook, *and a warm, witty woman with lots of good sense about food. Her book, by the way, is the best Italian cookbook I know of.*

In addition to writing, Marcella teaches weekly cooking classes in her apartment. One of the things she stresses to students is that Italian food should not be thought of as pasta and sauces, but as nutritious, economical, and easy-to-prepare cuisine—of which her minestrone is an example. It's a favorite with all her students and I like it because it can either be made ahead of time or prepared right at the dinner hour. Either way, it's always good.

Makes 8 servings

- 2 pounds boiling potatoes, pared and roughly chopped
- 1 small onion, chopped (¼ cup)
- 3 tablespoons butter
- 4 tablespoons vegetable oil
- ¼ cup finely chopped carrot
- ¼ cup finely chopped celery
- ½ cup freshly grated parmesan cheese
- 2 cups milk
- 1 teaspoon salt
- 2 cups canned chicken broth, or more if a thinner soup is desired
- 3 tablespoons chopped parsley

1. Put potatoes in a large kettle or Dutch oven; add just enough water to cover. Bring to boiling; lower heat. Cover and cook until potatoes are tender, about 20 minutes. Mash potatoes with their liquid through a food mill back into the pot; reserve.
2. Put onion, butter, and oil into a pan and sauté until onion turns pale gold. Add carrot and celery and cook for 2 or 3 minutes, but not much longer or the vegetables will lose their crunchy consistency. Add vegetable mixture to potatoes.
3. Place kettle over medium heat, adding grated cheese, milk, salt, and sufficient broth to give the desired consistency. Bring to boiling; lower heat. Cook for 2 to 3 minutes, stirring constantly.
4. Off heat, stir in the chopped parsley. Serve with additional grated cheese on the side.

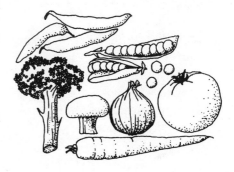

Brennan's Onion Soup au Gratin

It's a tradition in New Orleans to have breakfast at Brennan's; and this means not only eggs, but a bowl of their onion soup. The recipe for this French classic, which the restaurant's chef was kind enough to offer me, is unusual because of the egg yolks and cream added to the basic broth. The result is a uniquely delicious soup.

Makes 4 servings

   8 tablespoons (1 stick) butter
1½ cups thinly sliced white onions
   ½ cup all-purpose flour
   2 cans (13¾ ounces each) beef broth
1½ teaspoons salt
   Dash of cayenne
   1 egg yolk
   2 tablespoons light cream
   4 thin slices French bread
   ½ cup freshly grated parmesan cheese

1. Melt butter in a large, heavy saucepan. Sauté onions in butter until very soft. Blend in flour and cook for 5 minutes, stirring constantly. Stir in broth, salt, and cayenne.

2. Heat to boiling, stirring constantly. Lower heat; simmer for 15 minutes.
3. Beat egg yolk and cream in a small bowl; blend in about 1 cup of the hot soup. Stir mixture into saucepan.
4. Ladle soup into 4 individual heatproof bowls. Float a slice of French bread on each and top with parmesan cheese.
5. Broil, watching carefully, 4 inches from heat, just until cheese turns golden.

Coach House Black Bean Soup

"Every restaurant, whether it's a coffee shop or a fancy French establishment, needs a trademark—some special dish of its own by which the restaurant is known," says Leon Lianides, owner of New York's elegant Coach House Restaurant. What is the Coach House's trademark? Well, it's black bean soup, and it's an outstandingly different and delicious mixture that the restaurant traditionally serves with cornsticks oozing with a melted Roquefort cheese filling. Here's the recipe for this fragrant soup, thanks to Mr. Lianides' generosity.

Makes 8 servings

1 package (1 pound) black beans
2½ quarts (10 cups) water
5 strips bacon, cut in small pieces
2 stalks celery, chopped
2 medium onions, chopped (1 cup)
2 tablespoons flour
  Rind and bone from a smoked ham or 2 smoked ham hocks, split (about 1½ pounds)
3 pounds beef bones
3 sprigs Italian parsley
2 bay leaves
2 cloves garlic, halved
2 carrots, cut in pieces
2 parsnips, coarsely chopped
¼ teaspoon pepper
2 teaspoons salt
¾ cup madeira wine
2 hard-boiled eggs, finely chopped

1. Wash beans; cover with cold water and soak overnight. Drain and wash again. Place beans in a casserole; add water. Cover and simmer for about 90 minutes.
2. Cook bacon in a heavy kettle for a few minutes. Add celery and onion and cook until tender. Do not brown. Blend in flour and cook, stirring, for 1 minute. Add ham and beef bones, parsley, bay leaves, garlic, carrots, parsnips, pepper, salt, and beans with the cooking liquid. Cover and simmer over low heat, stirring occasionally, for 4 hours.
3. Add more water, if necessary. Remove bones and ham rind or hocks, and put soup through a sieve, straining thoroughly. Remove any meat from ham bone or hocks; chop meat finely and return to soup.
4. Reheat soup. Add madeira wine and eggs; mix well. Adjust salt and pepper. Serve hot; garnish each serving with a lemon slice sprinkled with parsley, if you wish.

Danish Yellow Pea Soup

When Mimi Sheraton reported on Danish cooking for a recent issue of Family Circle, *she included this soup in her story because it's one of the country's typical national dishes. But as Mimi notes, to call it "soup" is inadequate. It's a hearty meal-in-a-pot served with aquavit and beer and whole-grain black bread. And to be true to a Scandinavian tradition, follow it with three kinds of sliced meats (two are cooked right in the soup).*

Makes 8 to 10 servings

1 pound (2 cups) yellow split peas
5 cups water
1 teaspoon salt
1 pound lean, streaky salt pork, rinsed under cold water
2 pounds neck or shoulder of pork, rolled as for a roast
1 bay leaf
3 sprigs parsley
1 teaspoon leaf thyme, crumbled
2 leeks, well washed
3 stalks celery, sliced
1 parsnip, pared and diced
2 large carrots, scraped and sliced
2 large onions, diced, or 10 small white onions
4 medium potatoes, pared and cubed
1 pound medisterpølse (Danish sausages), German weisswürst, or smoked frankfurters

1. Wash peas and soak overnight in water. Drain. Add salt to water; bring to boiling. Add peas; lower heat. Simmer for about 1½ hours, or until tender, skimming skins and scum as they rise to surface. Puree peas through a sieve, blender, or food mill.

2. While peas cook, place salt pork and pork in a large saucepan. Add water to cover, about 6 to 7 cups. Bring to boiling; skim. Lower heat; add bay leaf, parsley, thyme, and one of the leeks, unsliced. Simmer 1½ hours. Then add celery, parsnip, carrots, the remaining leek (slice the white part only), onions, and potatoes. Cook 30 minutes longer, or until vegetables and meat are tender.

3. Remove meat and vegetables from broth. Cool broth; skim fat from surface. Gradually stir broth into pureed peas and simmer until thick and creamy. Add cooked vegetables to soup. Taste; add additional seasonings, if you wish.

4. Cook sausages. Slice salt pork and fresh pork and serve hot or cold with sausages, following the soup, along with mustard and pickled beets, if you wish.

Best of the Best Salads

The Four Seasons' Asparagus Vinaigrette
Maxwell's Plum Spinach, Bacon, and
 Mushroom Salad
California Caesar Salad
Peg Bracken's Sour Cream Cole Slaw
Nika Hazelton's Cucumber Salad
Swiss Potato Salad
Nika Hazelton's White-Bean Salad
Tex-Mex Guacamole Salad
Jean Anderson's Green Goddess Salad Dressing

The Four Seasons' Asparagus Vinaigrette

It has a beautiful view, a fine art collection, and an ultra modern decor complete with reflecting pool and windows curtained in burnished swag shades. There's none other like it. But on top of having a unique and very New York atmosphere, The Four Seasons also has one of the finest menus in town. It's always a treat to go there and sample their specialties such as this asparagus vinaigrette, which I've been using for many years.

Makes 8 servings

1 large bunch fresh asparagus (about 3 pounds) or 3 packages (10 ounces each) frozen asparagus spears
⅔ cup vegetable oil
½ cup wine vinegar
1 teaspoon salt
½ teaspoon sugar
¼ teaspoon pepper
1 tablespoon finely chopped capers
1 tablespoon finely chopped gherkins
1 tablespoon finely chopped pimiento
1 tablespoon finely chopped ripe olives
1 tablespoon finely chopped parsley

1. Wash and trim asparagus. Stand upright in a deep saucepan. Pour in boiling water to a depth of about 1 inch; cover. Cook for 15 minutes, or just until crisply tender. (If using frozen asparagus, follow the package directions.) Drain asparagus and arrange on a platter; cover with transparent wrap and chill.
2. Combine oil, vinegar, salt, sugar, and pepper in a jar with a screw top. Cover jar and shake well. Add capers, gherkins, pimiento, olives, and parsley. Shake again and chill at least 2 hours to develop flavors.
3. Divide asparagus spears among 8 chilled salad plates. Spoon dressing over asparagus and serve immediately.

Maxwell's Plum Spinach, Bacon, and Mushroom Salad

The bustling atmosphere at Maxwell's Plum has made it a popular spot with New York's café society, as well as with tourists from all over the country. But, with or without the atmosphere, the food still makes this one of the places to go when you're hungry. This is just one of their specialties and, to my mind, it's the best of all spinach, bacon, and mushroom salads.

Makes 6 servings

 1 pound fresh spinach
 6 slices bacon, cooked and crumbled (½ cup)
 ¼ pound large mushrooms, thinly sliced
 2 tablespoons red wine vinegar
 ¼ cup olive oil
 ½ teaspoon salt
 ¼ teaspoon pepper

1. Clean spinach and cut off stems up to leaf. Wash spinach three times in cold water; drain well. Place in salad bowl. Add bacon and mushrooms.
2. Combine vinegar, oil, salt, and pepper; pour over salad. Toss salad with dressing to coat evenly, just before serving.

California Caesar Salad

I can make a meal out of Caesar salad with a little wine and some crusty bread on the side. I also enjoy it as a first course, the way it is often served in restaurants, particularly in California, where it originated. This is Nika Hazelton's version of this now famous salad, and it's one I thoroughly enjoy.

Makes 6 to 8 servings

 2 cloves garlic
 ¾ cup olive oil
 2 cups bread cubes (4 slices)
 2 large or 3 small heads romaine lettuce
 ½ teaspoon pepper
 ½ teaspoon salt
 2 medium eggs, soft-cooked for 1 minute
 3 tablespoons lemon juice
 6 anchovy fillets, drained and cut into small pieces (optional)
 ½ cup freshly grated parmesan cheese

1. Cut one of the garlic cloves in half. Rub cut surface over inside of a large salad bowl. Discard. Brown remaining garlic clove in ¼ cup olive oil in a large skillet. Remove from oil. Add bread cubes; brown on all

sides. Drain croutons on paper toweling.

2. Break romaine leaves into bite-size pieces into salad bowl. Sprinkle with pepper and salt. Add remaining olive oil. Mix gently until every piece of lettuce is glistening with oil. Break eggs into the middle of the romaine and pour lemon juice directly over the eggs. Toss gently but thoroughly until there is a creamy look to the salad. Add the anchovies and cheese; taste, adding more salt, pepper, and lemon juice, if desired. (Go easy on the salt since the parmesan is salty.) Toss; add the croutons and toss again. Serve immediately so that the croutons remain crisp.

Peg Bracken's Sour Cream Cole Slaw

"My ideal recipe," says Peg Bracken, "is one that someone else locates and cooks. Second best is something that's hard to spoil, easy to make, and remarkably good tasting. This one qualifies." Need I say more?

Makes about 6 cups

1 large head cabbage
2 eggs
½ cup vinegar
1 tablespoon salt
1 tablespoon sugar
2 teaspoons dry mustard
¼ teaspoon pepper
2 cups dairy sour cream
2 cups finely sliced or shredded cucumber
¼ cup sliced green onion

1. Shred the cabbage and wash it all. Drain and chill.
2. Mix the eggs, vinegar, salt, sugar, mustard, and pepper together in a medium-size saucepan and cook over very low heat until thick. Cool and add the sour cream.
3. Add the cucumber and green onion to the cold, crisp cabbage and as much of the sour-cream dressing as you like. There will be more dressing than needed, so save it. (It's very good for potato salad, too.)

Nika Hazelton's Cucumber Salad

This cucumber salad was originally planned as part of a barbecue menu, complete with spitted roast of lamb, sourdough bread, cake, fruit, and wine. But because it's so refreshing, I like it with any outdoor meal— even if it's just steak or burgers.

Makes 4 to 6 servings

3 large cucumbers, peeled and thinly sliced
⅓ cup cider vinegar
2 tablespoons water
¼ cup sugar
1 teaspoon salt
¼ teaspoon pepper
1 tablespoon minced dill

1. Put cucumber slices into a bowl of water and ice cubes. Refrigerate for 1 hour. Drain; pat dry with paper toweling. Arrange in serving bowl.
2. Combine vinegar, water, sugar, salt, and pepper. Pour mixture over cucumbers. Refrigerate at least 1 hour. At serving time, drain off liquid; sprinkle with dill.

Swiss Potato Salad

When you look at the selection of recipes in the vegetable chapter, you'll see potatoes are one of my weaknesses. I've tried lots of salads made with this good old reliable, but this is still one of my favorites. Nika Hazelton gave me the recipe and she suggests serving the salad at room temperature. So after it's fixed, don't chill it at all; let it stand in a cool spot until serving time. What could be easier!

Makes 6 servings

12 medium potatoes
2 cans (10½ ounces each) condensed beef consommé or condensed chicken broth, diluted as label directs
⅓ cup dry white wine
⅓ cup olive or salad oil
2 tablespoons wine or cider vinegar (or more to taste)
1 teaspoon salt
Pepper
¼ cup drained capers, chopped
⅓ cup minced parsley

1. Scrub potatoes with a stiff brush; place them in a deep saucepan. Add beef consommé or chicken broth. Heat to the

boiling point. Lower heat and simmer until potatoes are tender. Drain potatoes and peel. While still warm, and this is very important, slice potatoes into a bowl and sprinkle with wine. Cool to room temperature.

2. Combine oil, vinegar, salt, and pepper; mix well. Sprinkle dressing over potatoes; add capers. Toss carefully with two forks, being careful not to break potato slices. Sprinkle parsley over top.

Nika Hazelton's White-Bean Salad

One thing I admire about good cooks is their adaptability. In a pinch they can find a substitute for an ingredient they don't have, or take an effective short-cut if time is a problem.

This is one of the reasons I like so many of Nika Hazelton's recipes. If she lists a start-from-scratch ingredient or one that may be hard to find, she'll often give an alternate choice—an ingredient that's time-saving or more readily available. In

this white-bean salad, for instance, the recipe calls for cooking your own dried navy beans. But Nika says it can also work well if you start with the canned variety that you only have to drain and rinse in cold water before adding to the other ingredients.

Makes 6 servings

4 cups freshly cooked white navy beans or 2 cans (1 pound, 4 ounces each) cannellini (white kidney beans)
½ cup olive oil
¼ cup lemon juice
Salt
Pepper
4 scallions or green onions, trimmed and chopped
2 tomatoes, sliced
2 hard-boiled eggs, quartered

1. Place beans in a deep bowl. Combine olive oil, lemon juice, salt, and pepper; mix well. Pour over beans. Cover and let stand for 4 hours, or overnight, to season.

2. At serving time, drain beans; fold in scallions. Spoon beans into a serving dish and garnish with alternate slices of tomatoes and quarters of hard-boiled eggs.

Tex-Mex Guacamole Salad

I used to think guacamole was strictly a dip. But as Nika Hazelton points out, this Tex-Mex favorite also makes a colorful salad when served with chopped tomatoes and corn chips. It's a nice way to vary a good thing.

Makes 4 cups

  2 large, ripe avocados (approximately ¾ pound each)
  3 tablespoons lemon juice
  1 teaspoon salt
  ⅛ teaspoon pepper
  1 tablespoon grated onion
  1 4-ounce can hot, green chili peppers, seeded and chopped

1. Cut avocados in half; remove pits and peel. Mash with lemon juice until smooth in a large bowl. Add salt, pepper, onion, and hot peppers.
2. Serve with peeled chopped tomatoes and corn chips, if you wish.

Jean Anderson's Green Goddess Salad Dressing

Like many fine cooks, Jean Anderson is a collector of recipes, including some terrific ones she develops herself. But when Jean collects recipes they usually end up in cookbooks and magazine articles—rather than the usual kitchen file box. This delicious salad dressing recipe is one she created and, true to style, here it is in a cookbook—for posterity and lots of good eating.

Makes about 3 cups

  ⅓ cup tarragon vinegar
  1 cup mayonnaise
  1 cup dairy sour cream
  ⅓ cup minced fresh tarragon
  ½ cup minced fresh parsley
  3 tablespoons minced fresh chives
  2 tablespoons anchovy paste
    Juice of ½ lemon
  1 clove garlic, peeled and crushed
    Pepper

Blend all the ingredients together, cover and chill 1 to 2 hours. Use to dress crisp greens.

Note: This dressing will keep well in the refrigerator for about a week in a tightly covered glass jar.

Best of the Best Main Dishes

Romeo Salta's Straw and Hay
Jack Kelleher's Veal Kidneys with Cream
Jane O'Keefe's Roast Fresh Ham with
    Cumberland Sauce
Maxwell's Plum Shish Kabob
Trader Vic's Indonesian Lamb Roast
Coach House Rack of Lamb
Coach House Chicken Pie
Sardi's Deviled Roast Beef Bones
The Four Seasons' Steak Tartare
The Four Seasons' Carpaccio
John Clancy's Foolproof Beef Stroganoff
John Clancy's Sensational Stuffed Pork Chops
The Best Corned Beef Hash
The London Chop House Tournedos aux
    Champignons
Wintertime Steak au Poivre
Nika Hazelton's Steak Sauce and Butters
Hamburger "21"
Myra Waldo's Brazilian Hamburgers
Danny Dickman's Steak Diane Flambé
Craig Claiborne's Real Texas Chili
Jean Hewitt's Barbecued Spareribs

Empress of China Beef

Virginia Lee's Crisp Fried Fish with Sweet and
Sour Sauce

Virginia Lee's Kung Pao Beef

Captain Ebanks' Fish Stew

Mrs. Oscar McCollum's Southern Fried Chicken

Mrs. McCollum's Pork Sausage and Tomato Pies

Canadian Pork Pie

Florence Lin's Stir-Fried Pork with Peppers

Horikawa's Sukiyaki

Horikawa's Tempura

Grace Chu's Shrimp Chop Suey

Madame Chu's Orange Leek Duck

"21" Club Duckling Bigarade

Lena Erculiani's Chicken Cacciatora

Ann Seranne's Roast Prime Ribs of Beef

Ann Seranne's Baked Lobster

Ann's Roast Turkey with All the Trimmings

Ann's Poached Chicken with Lemon Sauce

Zesty Welsh Rabbit

Helen McCully's Veal Cordon Bleu

Helen McCully's Coq au Vin

Perla Meyers' Cassoulet

Frogs' Legs Provençale with Tomatoes
Concasser from La Grenouille

Mefr's Oyster Stew a la "Souper Bowl"

Oyster Bar Fried Clams

Marian Burros' Butterflied Leg of Lamb
for the Outdoor Grill

Diana Kennedy's Swiss Chard Enchiladas

Sheryl Julian's Gougère with Mushrooms and Ham

Marcella Hazan's Ziti with Sausage and
    Cream Sauce
Marcella Hazan's Tripe and Beans
Marcella Hazan's All-Seafood Fish Soup
Veal Scallopine with Marsala and Cream
Marcella Hazan's Fricasseed Chicken with Lemon
Marcella's Spaghetti with Fish-Head Soup
Fillet of Beef Wellington
Josette King's Spinach and Egg Casserole

Romeo Salta's Straw and Hay (Green & White Pasta)

Of all the restaurants I've been to, there's none I feel more welcome in than Romeo Salta. It's because Romeo is so hospitable and makes everyone who comes into his New York establishment feel relaxed and at home. His restaurant is also, in my humble opinion, the best Italian restaurant this side of Ristorante Sabatini in Florence. The reason is obvious. Romeo takes his business seriously and, as he points out, running a great restaurant is not fun and games.

He has spent years learning his trade and teaching it to his children, one of whom he recently sent to Sabatini's for a year's apprenticeship; and that means learning the best from the best. Romeo works crazy hours, too. He's up at 4 in the morning, on his feet all day, with a nap at 5 or 6 in the evening, and then back to work until late at night, which convinced me that running this kind of business is not done just for money. You really have to love food.

This recipe for straw and hay or, in Italian, paglia e fieno papalina, *is a good example of the kind of entrée Romeo serves: superb!*

Makes 4 main-dish servings, or 6 first-course servings

½ pound Egg Pasta (recipe follows) or 1 8-ounce package medium egg noodles
½ pound Green Pasta (recipe follows) or 1 8-ounce package green egg noodles
1 pound mushrooms
4–6 tablespoons butter
1 clove garlic
Salt
Pepper
½ pound prosciutto, minced
1 cup light cream
½ cup freshly grated parmesan cheese

1. Prepare egg pasta and green pasta and allow to rest for 30 minutes. Cut into tagliatelle or tagliolini (thick or thin ribbon noodles) and allow to dry on a large clean cloth.
2. Wipe mushrooms with a damp cloth and slice. Melt half the butter in a deep skillet; sauté garlic gently, until brown, then remove. Add mushrooms and season with salt and pepper. Sauté for 10 minutes; keep hot.
3. Melt remaining butter in a second skillet. Add prosciutto and brown; keep hot.
4. Heat cream in a bain-marie or in the top of a double boiler over simmering water.
5. Bring two kettles of salted water to the boil. Add egg pasta

to one kettle and green pasta to the other and return to boiling; test. Pasta should be tender, yet firm; drain. (If using packaged noodles, follow label directions; then drain.)

6. Combine noodles in a heated large deep platter. Add mushrooms, prosciutto, cream, and parmesan cheese; toss until well coated and serve immediately.

Egg Pasta

Makes about 1 pound

- 3 cups sifted all-purpose flour
- 2 teaspoons salt
- 3 eggs
- 2 tablespoons olive or vegetable oil
- ¼ cup lukewarm water

1. Sift flour and salt onto a large wooden board; make a well in center. Add eggs, oil, and water. Work liquids into flour with fingers to make a stiff dough. (Or make dough in a large bowl, but it's not as much fun.)
2. Knead dough on board (do not add additional flour) for 10 minutes, or until dough is smooth and soft. Wrap dough in plastic wrap. Let stand for 30 minutes. Cut into quarters; keep each quarter of dough wrapped until ready to roll out, or it will dry out.

3. Roll' out dough quarter on wooden board to a 10-by-8 rectangle. (Do not use additional flour, but if dough really sticks, sprinkle board lightly with cornstarch.) This takes a lot of pressure. Cut dough with a sharp knife into tagliatelle or tagliolini (thick or thin ribbon noodles). Repeat with remaining dough.
4. Allow to dry on a clean cloth for at least 1 hour. Noodles are now ready to be cooked in a large kettle of boiling salted water. (Or they may be wrapped in plastic wrap and stored in the freezer for future use.) Remember, homemade noodles cook much more quickly than packaged ones. They should be tender, yet firm. Drain immediately.

Green Pasta

Follow directions for egg pasta, substituting 1 package (10 ounces) frozen, chopped spinach, cooked, drained, and pureed for the ¼ cup lukewarm water.

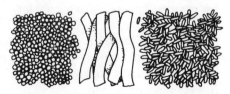

Jack Kelleher's Veal Kidneys with Cream

When Jack Kelleher calls and says, "come on over, I'm making kidneys on toast," I go. Because like most things he cooks, this is fantastic. Besides, Jack is a knowledgeable man with a salty character and warm Irish humor. He's also, as unlikely as it may seem, an avid Francophile, particularly when it comes to food. He just loves anything French, and when he's not busy with his executive responsibilities at Macy's, Jack can often be found cooking up one of his specialties and practicing his French at the same time. He's taught himself both, and he's done a bang-up job of it!

Makes 4 servings

- 4 **veal kidneys or 8–12 lamb kidneys**
- 3–4 **tablespoons unsalted butter**
- 1 **tablespoon finely chopped shallots**
- ½ **cup Beef Stock (recipe follows)**
- ½ **cup dry white wine (burgundy —pinot chardonnay type)**
- 2 **tablespoons cognac**
- 1 **tablespoon Dijon mustard (Maille is OK)**
- 2 **tablespoons cornstarch**
- 1 **cup heavy cream**
  Salt
  Pepper
  Unbuttered toast

1. Peel off membranes, if still on veal or lamb kidneys. Trim off fat and cut veins from under sides.
2. Sauté kidneys in butter in a large heavy skillet, turning often, for 10 minutes, or just until tender, but still slightly pink near center. Remove and keep warm.
3. Stir shallots into skillet and sauté for 1 minute; stir in beef stock and wine. Cook, stirring up all the cooked juices in bottom of pan, until mixture becomes syrupy.
4. Warm cognac in a small metal cup; ignite and pour into pan. Stir until flames die out.
5. Blend mustard with cornstarch and cream in a small bowl until well blended.
6. Cut kidneys into ¼-inch thick slices; reserve juices.
7. Stir cream mixture into skillet and cook, stirring constantly, until bubbly. Add kidneys and juices; taste and season with salt and pepper. Cook just until sauce thickens. Spoon over toast on heated serving plates and serve immediately.

Jack Kelleher's Beef Stock

Makes 12 cups

1 pound beef rump
1½ pounds beef or veal knuckle bones
1 large carrot, scraped and cut into chunks
3 large onions
3 whole cloves
1 stalk celery with leaves, cut into chunks
2 leeks, well washed and chopped
3 sprigs parsley
2 cloves garlic
½ bay leaf
¼ teaspoon leaf thyme, crumbled
¼ teaspoon leaf rosemary, crumbled
12 cups water

1. Combine beef rump, bones, carrot, onions (one studded with whole cloves), celery, leeks, parsley, garlic, bay leaf, thyme, rosemary, and water in a stock pot or large kettle.
2. Bring to boiling. Lower heat and simmer for 6 hours. Cool; remove fat layer and reheat to boiling. Strain through cheesecloth into a large bowl.
3. Cool; then refrigerate.

Note: To freeze, pour cooled stock into plastic freezer containers in recipe-size portions. Label, date, and freeze. Use within 4 months.

Jane O'Keefe's Fresh Roast Ham with Cumberland Sauce

Fresh ham, or roasted leg of pork as it's sometimes called, is a traditional holiday favorite. It's a shame, however, that this is the only time some people prepare it. I think it should be enjoyed year-round (but then I feel that way about turkey too), particularly when you have a recipe as good as this one. It was given to me by Jane O'Keefe, director of Family Circle's *Test Kitchens, and Jane recommends serving the roast with a cumberland sauce. Made with madeira and currant jelly, the sauce is a welcome change from the usual brown meat gravy. But with or without gravy, the roast is superb.*

Note: I especially love to roast fresh ham on the outdoor barbecue spit. And, to tell you the truth, I don't bother with the sauce outdoors, but serve applesauce with it instead. The crackly skin of the outdoor version is unbeatable.

Makes 12 to 16 servings

1 leg of pork (fresh ham), 10–15 pounds, with skin (rind)
2 teaspoons salt
½ teaspoon pepper
1 large onion, sliced
6 medium baking potatoes, quartered lengthwise
Cumberland Sauce (recipe follows)

1. Score skin in small diamond pattern. Rub with salt and pepper. (When roasted, the skin will be crackly and brown.)
2. Put meat in roasting pan. If using roast thermometer, insert into thickest part of meat so bulb is not touching bone or resting in fat.
3. Roast at 325 degrees for 25 minutes per pound. One hour before the end of roasting time, pour off all drippings from pan. Measure and return ¼ cup to pan; reserve all remaining drippings for sauce. Remove rack from pan. Add onions and potatoes; continue roasting, turning potatoes once or twice until roast and potatoes are done.
4. Meanwhile, make cumberland sauce to serve with roast. Serve potatoes with roast, and garnish platter with watercress and grilled orange slices, if you wish.

Cumberland Sauce

Makes 1⅔ cups

Roast pork pan juices, 1 cup
2 oranges
⅓ cup orange juice
2 tablespoons cornstarch
1 cup ruby port
½ cup currant jelly
5 drops Tabasco

1. Skim fat from reserved pan juices; discard fat. Add water, if necessary, to make 1 cup pan juice.
2. Pare thin orange zest from both oranges; parboil for 5 minutes. Cut into thin shreds. Squeeze oranges to yield ⅓ cup juice.
3. Stir cornstarch into orange juice in medium-size saucepan. Stir in port, currant jelly and Tabasco. Bring to boiling, stirring constantly. Cook until bubbly and then cook 1 minute longer. Stir in orange rind. Serve with pork.

Maxwell's Plum Shish Kabob

When brought to your table atop a serving of Rice Istanbul, with a broiled tomato and lemon garnish on the side, the shish kabob at Maxwell's Plum is a sight to behold. No wonder it's one of the most popular entrées served at this familiar New York spot. But it's also nice to be able to enjoy such fare at home once in a while. Thanks to the chef at Maxwell's Plum, this is possible because here's the recipe for the shish kabob and the rice.

Makes 6 servings

1 medium onion, sliced
3 cloves garlic, crushed
1 cup chopped celery
¼ teaspoon cumin seed
1 cup cider vinegar
1 cup lemon juice
½ cup vegetable oil
1 teaspoon salt
¼ teaspoon pepper
½ leg of lamb (butt end), approximately 2½ pounds
2 large onions, cut in 1½-inch pieces
6 medium mushroom caps
6 green peppers, halved, seeded, and quartered
Rice Istanbul (recipe follows)

1. Make a marinade by combining sliced onion, garlic, celery, cumin, vinegar, lemon juice, oil, salt, and pepper in a medium-size bowl.
2. Bone the lamb; cut meat into 1-inch cubes. Place in a glass or ceramic dish. Pour marinade over lamb; cover. Refrigerate for 24 hours.
3. Blanch onion pieces in boiling water for 5 minutes; drain.
4. Thread a mushroom, pepper, and onion piece on long skewers alternately with 5 pieces of the marinated lamb.
5. Broil kabobs, 4 inches from heat, for 5 minutes. Turn; baste with marinade. Broil for 5 minutes; turn, and broil 5 minutes longer. Serve kabobs on Rice Istanbul. Garnish platter with a broiled tomato basket and a lemon basket with parsley, if you wish.

Rice Istanbul

Makes 6 servings

1 chicken liver
2 teaspoons butter
1 large onion, chopped
2 tablespoons vegetable oil
2 tablespoons shelled, blanched almonds, slivered

2 tablespoons golden raisins
2 cups rice
4 cups water
¼ teaspoon anise seeds
2 teaspoons salt
¼ teaspoon pepper
   Pinch of saffron
2 tablespoons melted butter
2 tablespoons diced pimiento

1. Sauté chicken liver in 2 teaspoons butter in a heatproof baking dish or skillet. Remove; chop.
2. In same dish sauté onion in 1 tablespoon of the oil until brown. Add almonds to onion and sauté until almonds brown. (This is a very important step.)
3. Add chicken liver, raisins, and rice. Mix together for about ½ minute; pour in water, anise seeds, salt, pepper, saffron, and remaining oil.
4. Stir once, bring to boiling, cover, and put into a moderate oven, 350 degrees, for 30 minutes, or until water is absorbed. Or leave baking dish or skillet on heat; cover, lower heat, and simmer for 30 minutes, or until rice is tender.
5. Remove from heat and put on a platter. Pour melted butter over top and stir with fork. Sprinkle pimientos over rice.

Trader Vic's Indonesian Lamb Roast

Trader Vic's is well known around the country for its entertaining and exotic Polynesian atmosphere as well as its varied menu—which, incidentally, includes some very potent drinks! This is perhaps one of the most famous of its entrées and was given to me by the chef at the San Francisco Trader Vic's.

Makes 8 servings

⅓ cup finely chopped celery
⅓ cup finely chopped onion
1 clove garlic, minced
½ cup vegetable oil
¼ cup cider vinegar
½ cup prepared mustard
3 tablespoons curry powder
1 teaspoon leaf oregano, crumbled
2 bay leaves
3 tablespoons honey
2 teaspoons grated lemon rind
3 tablespoons lemon juice
2 teaspoons bottled meat sauce
2 dashes Tabasco
8 thick rib or shoulder lamb chops, or a rack of lamb, trimmed of fat

1. Sauté celery, onion, and garlic in oil in a medium-size saucepan until onion is transparent. Stir in all remaining ingredients except meat. Simmer a few minutes, cool, and chill briefly.
2. Arrange chops in a shallow glass dish; pour marinade over. Let stand 3 to 4 hours, turning several times.
3. Drain chops. Wrap ends of rib chop bones with foil to keep from charring when broiling. Arrange chops on rack in broiler pan; brush with marinade.
4. Broil, with tops 4 to 5 inches from heat, for 4 minutes. Turn; brush again with marinade. Broil 4 minutes longer, or until meat is done to your taste. (Do not overcook—lamb is delicious and juicy when cooked to the "pink" stage.)
5. Pour off any excess oil from marinade, then heat remainder to serve as a sauce for chops and rice.

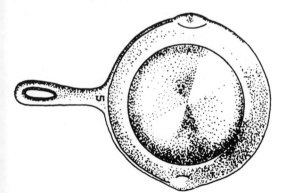

Coach House Rack of Lamb

For traditional American fare, there is no finer place in the entire country than the Coach House Restaurant in New York's Greenwich Village. For years they've had a distinguished reputation for quality food, simply prepared and beautifully served. The surroundings—fresh flowers, soft lighting, and priceless paintings—are also conducive to an enjoyable dining experience. In short, I like the place.

Two of the dishes that appear regularly on the menu and that owner Leon Lianides says are especially popular with the restaurant's clientele are the rack of lamb and chicken pie. Both are favorites of mine, too. The lamb, unlike others I've tried, is prepared by rubbing it with a little lemon juice, French olive oil, and parsley, and then roasting it at a high temperature. It's usually served with Bordelaise sauce and fresh artichoke hearts on the side. The chicken pie is also unique, made with a rich pie crust filled with chunks of chicken and just the right balance of vegetables. When you try these recipes, I feel confident you'll agree the Coach House has earned its reputation.

Makes 4 to 6 servings
(2 or 3 chops each)

2 6-chop racks of lamb, approximately 2 pounds each
1 clove garlic
½ teaspoon lemon juice
1 teaspoon good quality olive oil
¼ teaspoon salt
⅛ teaspoon pepper
2 teaspoons finely chopped parsley
Bordelaise sauce (recipe follows)

1. Remove all excess fat from meat; scrape ends of bones of all fat and meat, or have the butcher prepare the racks oven ready. (Any extra bits of meat may be used for making a hearty scotch broth, if you wish.)
2. Prepare Bordelaise sauce. Preheat oven to extremely hot, 500 degrees.
3. Crush garlic clove and rub over the bone side of the meat; discard clove.
4. Rub meat all over with lemon juice, then with olive oil. Sprinkle with salt and pepper; rub in parsley.
5. Put racks in roasting pan, meat side up. Roast for 10 minutes; turn. Roast for 10 minutes longer, or until lamb is browned on the outside, but still pink inside.

6. Cut each rack of 6 chops into 3 2-chop sections. Serve with Bordelaise sauce.

Bordelaise Sauce

Makes about 1½ cups

2 tablespoons finely chopped shallots
2 tablespoons butter
¾ cup dry red wine
1½ cups brown sauce or 1 10½-ounce can beef gravy
2 teaspoons lemon juice
Salt
Pepper

1. Sauté shallots in butter in a medium-size saucepan until tender, but not brown. Add wine and boil down until quantity is reduced by half.
2. Stir in brown sauce or gravy and lemon juice. Add salt and pepper to taste. Heat sauce to boiling; lower heat. Simmer for 5 minutes.

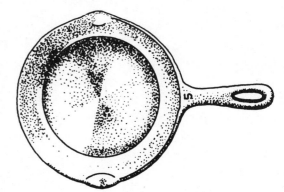

Coach House Chicken Pie

Makes 6 servings

1 roasting chicken (4½–5 pounds)
2½ quarts water
1 clove garlic, crushed
4 peppercorns
1 celery stalk with leaves, coarsely chopped
1 large onion studded with 4 whole cloves
1 tablespoon salt
3 carrots, scraped and cut into 1-inch pieces
12 small white onions
4 large fresh mushrooms
12 tablespoons (1½ sticks) butter
⅔ cup all-purpose flour
½ cup cooked or canned peas
1 tablespoon chopped parsley
1 Rich Piecrust (recipe follows)
1 egg yolk
1 tablespoon cream

1. Rinse and dry chicken. Bring water to boiling over high heat in a large kettle. Add chicken to the kettle with garlic, peppercorns, and celery. Add onion with cloves to kettle with salt. Lower heat; cover. Simmer chicken for about 1 hour and 20 minutes, or until tender. When done, leg will pull off easily.
2. Remove chicken from broth; cool. Remove celery and onion with slotted spoon; discard. Skim fat from broth.
3. Bring broth to boiling; add carrots, onions, and mushrooms. Remove mushrooms after 15 minutes of cooking; slice. Continue simmering carrots and onions until tender, about 5 minutes longer. Remove vegetables from broth; strain. Measure 4 cups broth; refrigerate remaining broth for another use.
4. Melt butter in a heavy skillet; stir in flour. Cook over medium heat, stirring constantly, for about 3 minutes, or until bubbly, but not brown. Gradually stir in the 4 cups broth. Cook, stirring constantly, until sauce thickens and bubbles for 1 minute. Remove from heat.

Season with salt and pepper to taste.

5. Remove chicken from bones; discard skin and bones. Cut chicken into fairly large pieces. There should be about 4 cups.

6. Pour half of sauce into bottom of a 12-cup, deep oval baking dish. Arrange the chicken, carrots, onions, and sliced mushrooms over the sauce. Sprinkle peas and parsley over; pour in remaining sauce. Refrigerate.

7. When ready to complete pie, roll out rich piecrust between 2 sheets of wax paper to about ¼-inch thickness. Measure dish; cut pastry to allow for a 1-inch overhang. Fit pastry over pie; turn edge under. Press pastry against side of dish with fork to seal. Cut steam vents in pastry. Cut leaves and flowers from pastry trims, if you wish. Arrange on top of pastry, moistening them with a little water so they adhere. Combine egg yolk and cream; brush pastry and decorations well with mixture.

8. Bake in hot oven, 400 degrees, for 45 minutes, or until crust is a deep, golden brown and filling is bubbly. Serve with salad.

Rich Piecrust

1½ cups sifted all-purpose flour
8 tablespoons (1 stick) butter, softened
1 egg yolk
1 teaspoon ice water

1. Place flour in center of a pastry board; make a well in center. Cut in the butter. Add egg yolk and ice water.

2. Work mixture together with fingers until well-blended. Form into ball; wrap in wax paper. Refrigerate before rolling out.

Sardi's Deviled Roast Beef Bones

Sardi's is one of New York's most celebrated gathering spots for theater people—and for people just going to the theater. It's also the place that serves one of my all-time favorite dishes—deviled roast beef bones.

Makes 2 servings

 4 beef bones from a cooked standing roast beef
 2 teaspoons dry English mustard
 ½ cup water
 ¾ cup bread crumbs
 4 tablespoons Deviled Sauce (recipe follows)

1. Blend mustard and water together. Dip bones into the mixture, covering well, and then dip into the bread crumbs.
2. Place in a shallow baking pan and broil until brown and hot, turning occasionally, for about 7 minutes. Serve with deviled sauce and decorate with watercress, if you wish.

Note: Rib bones can be saved from several roasts.

Deviled Sauce

Makes 1¼ cups

 ½ cup sherry wine
 ¼ cup prepared French mustard
 1¼ cups Brown Sauce, freshly made (recipe follows) or canned

1. Heat sherry in saucepan and reduce for 10 minutes. Add mustard. Simmer for 5 minutes. Add brown sauce and simmer for 5 minutes.
2. Serve hot on broiled meats or barbecues. This can be stored in the refrigerator for one week and reheated.

Brown Sauce

Makes 1¼ cups

 1½ tablespoons butter
 2 tablespoons flour
 1½ cups beef consommé
 ¼ cup sherry wine
 1 bay leaf
 ⅛ teaspoon commercial caramel coloring

1. Melt butter. Add flour. Mix well over heat for 1 minute, browning the flour slightly. Slowly add hot consommé, stirring all the time. Cook and stir for 2 minutes.

2. Add sherry wine and bay leaf. Boil gently for 15 minutes. Add caramel coloring. Bring to a boil and strain through a fine sieve. Sauce can be stored in refrigerator for about 1 week.

The Four Seasons' Steak Tartare

Paul Kovi and Tom Margittai are running one of the great restaurants of the world—The Four Seasons. They serve a rich array of delectable dishes and their dessert tray is almost irresistible. But one of my favorite dishes is a down-to-earth one—steak tartare. Here is their recipe.

Makes 3 or 4 servings

  2 **pounds fresh, lean, top round roast**
½ **lemon wedge**
  1 **small white onion, washed and very finely chopped**
2½ **tablespoons finely chopped fresh parsley**
1½ **teaspoons English or Dijon mustard**
1½ **teaspoons salt**
  1 **teaspoon pepper**
  2 **fresh raw egg yolks**
  3 **tablespoons cognac**

1. Use fresh lean meat only. Trim all fat from meat and wipe with a clean wet cloth. Cut into workable pieces and run it twice through a grinder with the medium blade.
2. Shape meat into a flat, round patty. Squeeze 10 to 12 drops lemon juice on meat. (If necessary, wrap it tightly in plastic or foil and refrigerate.)
3. Spread the chopped meat on the chopping board and blend in the onions with two forks. Fold the meat in from the edge to the center, spread out again, and mix in 2 tablespoons parsley. Follow same routine with mustard, salt, pepper, and egg yolks. Fold again, spread; add cognac. Fold once more, then work ingredients thoroughly into the meat.
4. Form meat into oval-shaped patties. Carefully smooth out all surfaces with a dinner knife. Sprinkle on top of each the remaining parsley, and eat as a main dish with a few crisp fresh vegetables and a little black bread.

The Four Seasons' Carpaccio

At Harry's Bar in Florence they serve a fantastic dish called carpaccio. *I'd never encountered it before going there last year. But now The Four Seasons, always alert to great food, is serving their version of* carpaccio. *It's every bit as good as Harry's Bar, and owner Paul Kovi was nice enough to give me his recipe for it.*

Makes 1 serving

2 slices (3½ ounces each) sirloin
    tartare (raw sirloin)
    Salt
    Pepper
    Sauce (recipe follows)

1. Place meat between two sheets of slightly oiled wax paper and pound with a mallet until wafer thin.
2. Transfer meat to a dinner plate. Sprinkle lightly with salt and pepper. Serve with sauce as an accompaniment.

Sauce

6 tablespoons mayonnaise
1 tablespoon brandy
1 teaspoon Dijon mustard

1. Blend together all ingredients.
2. Serve with carpaccio.

John Clancy's Foolproof Beef Stroganoff

If you want a good recipe for almost anything, John Clancy is the person to ask. He's an inventive cook and, as one of America's foremost cooking and baking teachers, his knowledge is unquestionable and his credentials extensive. He was the executive chef of the Foods of the World Cookbook *series (Time-Life, Inc.) and was responsible for supervising the adaptation and testing of all the recipes in the twenty-seven volumes on international cuisine. On top of that, John is the author of three best-selling cookbooks, is a popular food lecturer, and a former chef at New York's Coach House Restaurant.*

Personally, I enjoy his recipes because they're always easy to follow. The two I've included here are particularly simple because John originally wrote them specifically for beginning cooks. So if you've ever been behind a stove, how can you miss!

Makes 4 servings

1½ pound boneless sirloin steak (cut ½ inch thick)
1½ cups sour cream
4 teaspoons flour
2 tablespoons prepared mustard
1½ teaspoons salt
½ teaspoon sugar
½ teaspoon pepper
½ pound fresh mushrooms
2 large onions
4 tablespoons oil

1. Place steak in the freezer for about 30 minutes to firm the meat and make it easier to slice.
2. While meat chills, prepare sauce. In a medium-size bowl, blend sour cream, flour, mustard, salt, sugar, and pepper. Set aside.
3. Wipe mushrooms with damp paper towels; slice thinly. Peel and thinly slice onions. Heat 2 tablespoons oil in a heavy 10-inch skillet (or electric skillet set at 375 degrees) until very hot. Add onions and mushrooms and stir; reduce heat to low, 225 degrees. Cover pan; cook vegetables for 15 minutes.
4. While vegetables cook, remove meat from freezer and cut into ¼-inch strips, then cut strips into 2-inch lengths. Set aside.
5. Empty mushrooms and onions into a strainer set over a bowl. Wipe out the skillet with paper towels. Heat remaining oil in skillet until very hot. Add half the meat and toss the strips constantly with a wooden spoon

for 3 or 4 minutes, or until lightly browned. Remove to platter and brown remaining meat.

6. Put the meat and juices from the platter back into the skillet; stir in sour-cream mixture and drained vegetables from strainer. When mixture comes to a boil, cook for 2 minutes. Turn off heat. Serve the stroganoff with shoestring potatoes and buttered peas.

John Clancy's Sensational Stuffed Pork Chops

Makes 4 servings

3 tablespoons butter
1 green onion, finely chopped
½ cup dry bread crumbs
1 tablespoon snipped fresh parsley
¼ teaspoon salt
Dash of pepper
¼ teaspoon leaf rosemary, crumbled
4 center loin pork chops (cut 1 inch thick)
3 tablespoons oil
1 cup chicken broth
¼ cup white wine
2 teaspoons tomato paste

1. Melt butter in a small saucepan. Remove from heat. In a small bowl, combine green onion, bread crumbs, parsley, salt, pepper, and rosemary. Stir in melted butter with a fork to dampen crumb mixture.

2. Cut off all but a thin edge of fat from pork chops. Cut a pocket in each chop, then pack an equal amount of crumb mixture into each pocket, and secure the openings with skewers.

3. Heat oil in a heavy 10-inch skillet (or electric skillet set at 375 degrees until very hot. Add chops and sauté for about 4 minutes on each side, or until golden brown. Remove chops; pour off any fat, leaving the brown glaze in pan.

4. Add broth, wine, and tomato paste to skillet, stirring and scraping the bottom of the pan with a metal spatula to deglaze pan.

5. Lower heat and return chops to pan. Simmer, partially covered, for 10 minutes. Transfer chops to heated serving platter and cover with foil to keep warm. Raise the heat to high and boil down the sauce to about ½ cup. Turn off heat.

6. Spoon a little sauce over each chop. Garnish with cooked and buttered broccoli and carrots.

The Best Corned Beef Hash

Corned beef hash is a humble dish, but it has a unique and enjoyable flavor whether it's served for breakfast, lunch, or dinner. I like it, too, because I can't tell it's made from leftovers, which is more than I can say for many second-time-around meat and potato combinations. Whenever I have hash, this is the recipe I use. It's a reliable one and I recommend preparing it with poached eggs on top.

Makes 4 servings

  1 pound cooked, leftover, cold corned beef
  2 medium boiled potatoes, cold
  1 medium onion, coarsely chopped (½ cup)
  ¼ cup coarsely chopped green pepper
  1 teaspoon pepper
  4 tablespoons (½ stick) butter
  4 eggs

1. Put corned beef through food grinder, using coarse plate. Grind; measure. (There should be 3 cups coarsely ground corned beef.) Grind potatoes; measure. (There should be 1½ cups coarsely ground potatoes.)
2. Combine corned beef, potatoes, onion, the green pepper, and pepper in a large mixing bowl; mix thoroughly.
3. Slowly heat butter in a heavy 8-inch skillet until foamy.
4. Turn hash mixture into skillet, pressing down firmly with spatula or pancake turner.
5. Cook hash, uncovered, over medium heat for about 15 minutes, or until a brown crust forms on bottom. Turn with spatula so that some of the crust is brought to the top. Cook slowly, turning several times, until desired crust is formed, adding additional butter if necessary.
6. With the back of a spoon, make 4 shallow indentations on top of hash. Break an egg into each hollow. Cover; cook for 5 minutes, or to the firmness you desire. (Eggs should be soft enough to make a sauce for the hash.) Garnish with parsley. Serve with ketchup or chili sauce, if you wish.

The London Chop House Tournedos aux Champignons

The London Chop House is one of Detroit's finest restaurants and a place you should certainly try if you're a beef lover like me. They have an extensive meat selection and it's sometimes hard to choose which to order. But if you ask their chef, this is the one he'll often recommend.

Makes 2 servings

4 slices beef tenderloin (4 ounces each)
½ teaspoon salt
¼ teaspoon pepper
⅓ cup clarified butter
8 fresh mushrooms, sliced
3 shallots, chopped (2 tablespoons) or 2 whole scallions, chopped
½ cup dry sherry wine
⅓ cup heavy cream
1 tablespoon brandy

1. Heat a large skillet to very hot. Season the tenderloin slices on both sides with salt and pepper; pour butter into the skillet and place the tenderloins in the skillet. Sauté, turning once, to the desired doneness (preferably rare, which would be 2½ to 3 minutes to the side for about ½-inch thick slices). Remove from fire; transfer meat to preheated platters.

2. Add mushrooms and shallots to skillet and cook until gray. Add sherry and reduce over high heat until almost dry. Add cream and reduce until syrupy. Add brandy and pour over meat. Serve with potatoes.

Note: To clarify butter, melt 8 tablespoons (1 stick) butter in a small saucepan. Pour off clear yellow liquid (the clarified butter) and discard the milky solids remaining.

Wintertime Steak au Poivre

I'm one of those people who love to cook outdoors all year round. Barbecue cooking is even more fun in the winter time because it's slightly adventurous and out of the norm. And steak au poivre is perfect because it doesn't take too long.

Incidentally, I use as much pepper as possible on each side of the steak —it helps hold the juices in and makes the skin deliciously crusty.

Makes 6 to 8 servings

1 sirloin steak, 2 inches thick (approximately 4 pounds)
Cracked pepper
Salt

1. Wipe steak with damp paper toweling. Using your fingers and heel of hand, press cracked pepper into each side of the steak. Let stand at room temperature for 1 hour.
2. Grill about 5 inches from hot coals for about 8–10 minutes on each side for medium rare. Sprinkle with salt when removed from heat.

Note: To prepare in the broiler, broil for 15 minutes on the first side, 10 minutes on the second side, 4 inches from heat. For a further sophisticated touch, flame the steak. Transfer steak to a hot platter. Warm ¼ cup brandy; pour over steak and ignite.

Nika Hazelton's Steak Sauce and Butters

I'm an inveterate outdoor cooking buff—sometimes to the consternation of my family who don't always appreciate my erratic style with the barbecue. But steak and hamburgers are fairly foolproof, and to vary that fare I often use a special steak sauce or two butter combinations I got from Nika Hazelton.

Salsa Fria

Makes about 4 cups

2 pounds very ripe tomatoes
1 cup finely chopped onion
1–4 canned green chilis, finely. chopped (amount depends on degree of hotness desired)
2 tablespoons vegetable oil
1 teaspoon salt
¼ teaspoon pepper
   Chopped fresh coriander to taste or 1 teaspoon ground oregano
1–2 tablespoons cider vinegar (optional)

1. Dip tomatoes in boiling water for 15 seconds; slip off skins.
2. Chop tomatoes; combine with onion, chilis, oil, salt, pepper, coriander or oregano, and vinegar in a large bowl.
3. Cover; season in the refrigerator at least 2 hours. Serve chilled, with meats.

Maitre d'Hotel Butter

Makes about ⅔ cup

8 tablespoons (1 stick) butter, softened
2 tablespoons finely minced parsley
2 tablespoons finely minced chives
2 tablespoons lemon juice

1. Blend butter, parsley, and chives in a small bowl. Add lemon juice, a little at a time.
2. Turn out onto wax paper. Shape into a 1½-inch roll. Wrap tightly and refrigerate until firm. Cut into slices and serve 1 slice on each serving of meat.

Blue Cheese Butter

Makes about ¾ cup

½ cup blue or Roquefort cheese
4 tablespoons (½ stick) butter, softened
2 tablespoons sherry, white wine, brandy, or cream

1. Remove cheese and butter from refrigerator. Crumble the cheese. Allow both to stand at room temperature for about 2 hours, or until soft.
2. Mash cheese with butter in a small bowl. Use a fork first and then a spoon. Stir in sherry and mix to a smooth paste. Turn into a bowl and spoon over meats. (This may be prepared ahead of time and refrigerated, covered, and brought back to room temperature before serving.)

Hamburger "21"

A few years ago food writer and friend Barbara Kraus extorted this recipe from the late Bob Kriendler of "21," and I've been using it with great success ever since. This marvelous hamburger, incidentally, is probably the single most popular dish served at the elegant "21," at least at lunchtime. I use the mixture on the outdoor grill as well as inside.

Makes 4 servings

1 cup finely diced celery
6 tablespoons (¾ stick) butter
2 pounds ground beef round
2 eggs, beaten
2 teaspoons salt
¼ teaspoon pepper
½ cup water
1 teaspoon worcestershire sauce

1. Sauté celery in a small frying pan in 2 tablespoons of butter until soft.

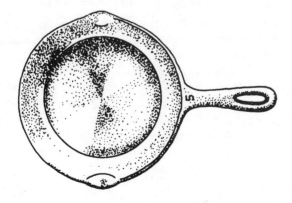

2. Combine ground beef, celery mixture, eggs, salt, pepper, water, and worcestershire sauce in a large bowl; mix lightly until well-blended. Shape into 4 large patties about 1 inch thick.
3. Sauté patties in remaining butter in a large frying pan for 5 minutes on each side for medium, or until done as you like. Serve with fresh green beans.

Myra Waldo's Brazilian Hamburgers

One of the first things I did as editor of Family Circle *was to call Myra Waldo for a story on international barbecues. As anyone who has read her travel books and best-selling cookbooks knows, she's an expert collector of recipes and fascinating facts about food. This is her recipe for Brazilian Hamburgers, and they're among the best I've tasted—north or south of the equator.*

Makes 8 servings

2 pounds ground beef
½ cup grated parmesan cheese
1 cup finely chopped green onions
1 cup finely chopped parsley
2 eggs, beaten
2 tablespoons water
1½ teaspoons salt
   Dash of cayenne

1. Mix all ingredients in a large bowl until well blended. Shape into 8 patties.
2. Place in a double-hinged wire broiling rack about 5 inches above hot coals. Grill, turning once to brown both sides, for 10 minutes, or until beef is done as you like it.

Danny Dickman's Steak Diane Flambé

After having tried numerous steak Diane recipes—most of them disappointing—I finally found one worth bragging about. It arrived on my desk not long ago as part of a series of recipes from four-star restaurants around the country. The story was written by Susanna Berger and she and I both agree that Danny Dickman, owner and chef of Danny's in Baltimore, knows how to prepare this tangy dish. This is Danny's favorite recipe, too, and it not only tastes spectacular, but it looks it!

Makes 2 servings

- 2 tablespoons clarified butter (see note)
- ¼ pound mushrooms, sliced
- 2 tablespoons chopped shallots or green onions
- ½ teaspoon chopped chives
- 1 teaspoon chopped parsley
- 2 mignonettes (fillets) of beef, about 4 ounces each (¾ to 1 inch thick)
- ¼ cup cognac
- ¼ teaspoon worcestershire sauce
- 1 tablespoon bottled meat sauce (Danny uses Escoffier-brand Sauce Robert)
- ¼ cup beef broth
- 2 tablespoons madeira or sherry
- ½ teaspoon salt
- ¼ teaspoon pepper

1. Pour butter into blazer pan of chafing dish (or use a 10-inch skillet). Heat, and when very hot (but not brown) add mushrooms, shallots, chives, and parsley. Cook, stirring constantly, for 2 minutes.
2. Add beef; cook for 2 minutes on each side.
3. Pour in cognac; warm gently, then ignite carefully. When flames die down, add worcestershire sauce and meat sauce.
4. Stir in broth, madeira, salt, and pepper. Cook for 2 minutes longer. Serve with wild rice, if you wish.

Note: To clarify butter, melt 2½ tablespoons butter in a small metal cup or saucepan. Pour off clear yellow liquid (the clarified butter) and discard the milky solids remaining.

Craig Claiborne's Real Texas Chili

Craig Claiborne's name is usually associated with sophisticated foods and the kind of haute cuisine he has written about as a reporter and food editor for the New York Times. *But Craig is also a chilihead, and he readily admits a lifelong addiction to the fiery stuff. Like so many chili lovers, he also never stops experimenting to find the ultimate recipe. So far, this one is his favorite.*

It's called Real Texas Chili because, as Craig explains, "the authentic Texas chili is a pure and unadulterated combination of beef, chili, garlic, cumin, oregano, and beef broth. And that's all." And when he says beef, he means chuck cut into small chunks, never ground beef— and no chopped vegetables either. Craig adds that when chili is served with beans, it's not called just chili, but chili con frijoles, *and he's included these as an optional ingredient. With or without them, this is still my favorite chili recipe too.*

Makes 8 servings

3 pounds boneless chuck, cut into 1-inch cubes
2 tablespoons vegetable oil
2–3 cloves garlic, chopped
4–6 tablespoons chili powder
2 teaspoons ground cumin
3 tablespoons flour
1 tablespoon leaf oregano
2 cans (13¾ ounces each) beef broth
1 teaspoon salt
¼ teaspoon pepper
1 15-ounce can pinto beans (optional)
1 cup dairy sour cream
1 lime, cut into wedges

1. Heat oil in 4-quart kettle or heavy-bottom pan over medium heat. Add beef, stirring frequently with a wooden spoon until meat changes color, but does not brown.
2. Lower heat; stir in garlic.
3. Combine chili powder, cumin, and flour. Sprinkle meat with chili mixture, stirring until meat is evenly coated. Crumble oregano over meat.
4. Add 1½ cans of broth and stir until liquid is well-blended. Add salt and pepper. Bring to a boil, stirring occasionally. Reduce heat; simmer, partially covered, over low heat, for 1½ hours. Stir occasionally. Add remaining broth; cook 30 minutes longer, or until meat is almost falling apart.

5. Cool thoroughly. Cover; refrigerate overnight to ripen flavor.
6. Reheat chili in top part of double boiler placed over boiling water.
7. If desired, heat beans, drain, and stir into chili. Garnish with sour cream and serve with wedges of lime to squeeze over each portion.

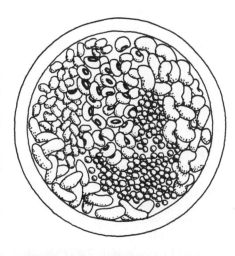

Jean Hewitt's Barbecued Spareribs

Whenever I have a cooking problem, I go straight to my favorite problem-solver and one of my favorite human beings, Jean Hewitt. When I asked her how to cook spareribs on the outdoor grill without burning them, she, as usual, had the solution: Line the grill with heavy-duty foil to make a shield between the fire and the ribs. The next weekend I cooked ribs, following this and her other special directions. And for the first time ever, they turned out perfectly!

Makes 6 servings as a main dish, or 12 servings as an appetizer

THE GRILL

If your barbecue grill is adjustable, fix it so the meat is 5 inches from the coals. If the grill isn't adjustable, use soup cans filled with stones or some other makeshift arrangement to keep the meat at this distance. An 18-inch-diameter grill will accommodate 2 racks of spareribs weighing 5½ to 6 pounds; a double hibachi will hold 1 rack. Cover the grill rack with heavy-duty aluminum foil; turn up the edges and make a trough down the center to catch the fat.

THE FIRE

Put a single uncrowded layer of charcoal in the firebox. Ignite the charcoal and allow it to reach the white ash stage—about 45 minutes. Scatter a handful of fresh charcoal over the hot coals; place the grill in position.

THE RIBS

Remove all excess fat from 2 whole racks, 2½ to 3 pounds each, of fresh spareribs, cracked but not severed down the middle. One pound serves 1 person as a main course, or serves 2 as an appetizer if they're cut in half lengthwise and then into smaller rib sections.

THE COOKING

1. Place the racks of ribs on the foil-lined grill over hot coals and cook, turning frequently, for about 45 minutes. Baste several times with beer, water, or chicken broth, and remove fat with spoon or bulb baster as it accumulates in the foil trough. At the end of 45 minutes, remove foil from grill.
2. Continue cooking the ribs on the bare grill until they are cooked through, about 45 minutes more. Keep turning and basting frequently with beer, water, or broth. If the fire flares up because of fat dripping, lift the ribs off with tongs, baste well and return to the grill when flames die down. Don't spray the fire with water; that cools down the fire and scatters a lot of ashes around. Test for doneness by cutting into the thickest part of the meat. There shouldn't be any pink color remaining. The out-side of the ribs should be the color of dark mahogany.
3. Transfer the ribs to a cutting board and hack with a cleaver or knife into individual ribs. Brush generously with spicy barbecue sauce (recipe follows). Return to the grill; turn ribs and brush second side and edges with sauce. Continue to cook, turning often and brushing with more sauce, until ribs are well-glazed — about 15 minutes longer. Serve immediately.

Spicy Barbecue Sauce

Makes about 2 cups

- 3 tablespoons vegetable oil (not olive oil)
- 1 extra-large onion, finely chopped (1½ cups)
- 2 cloves garlic, finely chopped
- 1 cup ketchup
- ½ cup wine vinegar
- ⅓ cup lemon juice
- ¼ cup worcestershire sauce
- ¼ cup brown sugar
- 4 teaspoons chili powder
- 2 teaspoons ground celery seeds
- 1 teaspoon ground cumin

1. Heat the oil in a large, heavy saucepan and sauté the onion slowly until golden and tender.

Add garlic and cook 1 minute longer.

2. Add ketchup, vinegar, lemon juice, worcestershire sauce, sugar, chili powder, celery seeds, and cumin.

3. Bring to boiling. Lower heat; simmer, uncovered, for 30 minutes. Brush on ribs.

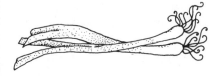

Empress of China Beef

The Empress of China Restaurant in San Francisco far surpasses what most people think of as a local Chinese restaurant. There are no plain tables and uninspired wall designs here, but rather an unforgettably beautiful atmosphere. The architecture and decor are those of the Han Dynasty (206 B.C.); many of the furnishings are antiques and the Empress Pavillon,, copied from the royal pleasure park in Peking, was built from old wood in Taiwan, then shipped and reassembled here. The food here is magnificent, too, and it's representative of the best Chinese cooking from every region of the nation. This dish, for instance, is a delicious import from Peking.

Makes about 4 servings

3 tablespoons vegetable oil
¼ teaspoon salt
½ pound boneless sirloin steak, cut into shoestring strips
1 large onion, thinly sliced
3 stalks celery, coarsely chopped (1 cup)
¼ pound fresh or frozen snow peas, each cut in half on a diagonal or ¼ pound frozen French-cut string beans (about ½ of a 10-ounce package)
1 3-ounce can whole mushrooms, drained and thinly sliced
½ cup coarsely chopped water chestnuts
1 tablespoon cornstarch
½ tablespoon sugar
5 tablespoons soy sauce
½ cup water

1. Heat oil in large skillet; add salt, then beef. Cook, stirring often, over high heat to brown meat, about 5 minutes. Add onion, celery, snow peas, mushrooms, and water chestnuts.

2. Continue cooking over high heat, stirring constantly for 2 to 3 minutes. Cover, lower heat, and simmer for about 3 minutes.

3. Combine cornstarch, sugar, soy sauce, and water in small dish; mix well. Add to skillet; cook, stirring constantly, until mixture thickens and bubbles for 1 minute. Serve immediately over fluffy, steamed rice.

Virginia Lee's Crisp Fried Fish with Sweet and Sour Sauce

The standard egg roll/fried rice/ chow mein combination seems dull when I think of Virginia Lee's cooking. Mrs. Lee is a renowned Chinese cooking teacher and co-author of The Chinese Cookbook *(with Craig Claiborne). And she's an expert on turning fantastic restaurant dishes into practical-size ones you can make at home. This dish is one of her specialties and I particularly like the recipe because I can get all the ingredients right in my supermarket.*

Makes 6 servings

1½ pounds fresh or partially thawed
    frozen flounder fillets
  1 teaspoon salt
 ½ teaspoon sugar
  1 tablespoon dry white wine or
    sherry
    Flour
  5 tablespoons cornstarch
  2 teaspoons baking powder
  1 teaspoon salt
  1 tablespoon vegetable oil
7–8 tablespoons water
    Oil for deep frying
    Sweet and Sour Sauce (recipe
    follows)

1. Wash fish; pat dry on paper towels. Cut into serving-size pieces; place in shallow dish. Dissolve salt and sugar in wine and sprinkle over fish to moisten evenly. Sprinkle flour onto wax paper; dip fish in flour to coat.
2. Combine 6 tablespoons flour, cornstarch, baking powder, salt, oil, and water in large bowl; stir with wire whisk until smooth. Dip fish in batter.
3. Put enough oil to make 2-inch depth in large skillet or dutch oven. Heat to 375 degrees on deep-fat frying thermometer. Lower fish, 2 to 3 pieces at a time, into hot oil. Cook, turning once or twice, until coating is golden brown and crisp, about 4 to 5 minutes. Drain on paper toweling. Keep warm. To serve, arrange fish on a deep platter. Spoon sweet and sour sauce over. Serve at once.

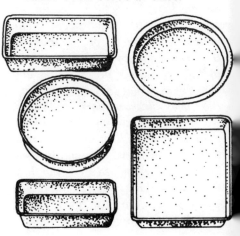

Sweet and Sour Sauce

4 Chinese mushrooms, soaked 30
minutes in hot water (see Note)
6 thin slices fresh ginger (see
Note)
3 cloves garlic, peeled and
smashed
1 medium onion, cut into ¾-inch
pieces
1 small carrot, thinly sliced
1 fresh red or green pepper,
seeded and cut into ¾-inch
pieces
1 fresh chili pepper, seeded and
cut into ¾-inch pieces (see
Note)
2 green onions, cut into 1½-inch
lengths
1 slice canned pineapple, cut into
chunks
1 cup water
⅓ cup cider vinegar
1 tablespoon soy sauce
½ cup sugar
1½ teaspoons salt
1 tablespoon cornstarch
2 tablespoons vegetable oil
Red food coloring (optional)

1. Squeeze excess water out of
mushrooms; slice crosswise.
Arrange prepared vegetables
and pineapple in separate
groups on a large plate.
2. Combine water, vinegar, soy
sauce, sugar, and salt in a 2-cup
measure. Stir to dissolve sugar.

Measure cornstarch into a small
bowl. Add 2 tablespoons of
vinegar mixture to cornstarch.
3. Heat oil in large saucepan; add
ginger, garlic, onion, and carrot;
stir fry for 15 seconds. Stir in
peppers, mushrooms, and pineapple; stir fry for 1 minute, or
until vegetables are crisply
done.
4. Add remaining vinegar mixture
to saucepan; bring to boiling.
Stir in cornstarch mixture and
green onion; boil for 1 minute.
Add 6 to 10 drops red food
coloring, if you wish. Serve over
fish.

Note: If fresh chili pepper is not
available, use canned chili
peppers or *jalapeños*; instead of
Chinese mushrooms, use fresh
mushrooms or canned mush-
rooms, drained; and in place of
fresh ginger, use candied ginger,
well washed.

Virginia Lee's Kung Pao Beef

In the last few years Chinese cooking has begun to receive the recognition it deserves, thanks to people like Virginia Lee. It's just surprising that it hasn't happened sooner since Chinese food is not only absolutely great, but often quite inexpensive. At any rate, here's another of Virginia's recipes, popular all by itself —and I enjoy it because it's on the hot side.

Makes 6 servings

- 1 pound flank steak
- 1 tablespoon cornstarch
- 2 tablespoons egg white
- 1 tablespoon vegetable oil
- 1 tablespoon soy sauce
- 2 green onions, cut into 1½-inch pieces
- 5 cloves garlic, peeled and smashed
- 4 thin slices fresh ginger root (see Note)
- 20 dried red pepper pods or 1 tablespoon crushed red pepper
- ½ cup dry-roasted peanuts
- 2 tablespoons dry white wine
- 2 tablespoons soy sauce
- 2 tablespoons cider vinegar
- 1½ teaspoons sugar
- 1 teaspoon salt
- 1½ teaspoons cornstarch
- 1 tablespoon water

- 2 cups vegetable oil
- 2 teaspoons sesame oil (optional)
- Hot fluffy rice

1. Cut flank steak in half lengthwise. With cleaver or heavy knife cut meat across the grain into slices ⅛-inch thick; place in large bowl. Add 1 tablespoon cornstarch, egg white, 1 tablespoon oil and 1 tablespoon soy sauce. Stir in one direction until meat is thoroughly coated.

2. Place on a platter large enough to hold remaining ingredients; refrigerate. Arrange the green onions, garlic, sliced ginger root, red pepper pods, and peanuts in separate groups on platter with meat.

3. Combine wine, 2 tablespoons soy sauce, vinegar, sugar, and salt in a small bowl. Combine 1½ teaspoons cornstarch with water in a cup.

4. Heat 2 cups oil in a wok or large skillet just until a piece of the meat bubbles when dropped in (about 280 degrees); add rest of the meat. Cook 1 minute, or just until steak strips are separated and lose most of their red color. Remove to a bowl with a slotted spoon. Carefully pour hot oil into a bowl; cool. Oil may be reused. This technique, known as "passing through," serves the purpose of separating the pieces of meat

at this lower temperature. When the meat is cooked at the higher stir-fry temperature, later in the recipe, it will remain separated.

5. Measure 2 tablespoons oil from the hot, drained oil into wok or skillet; place over medium-high heat. Add pepper pods or crushed red pepper; stir fry until pods are very dark to add an almost burned flavor. Rapidly stir in ginger, wine-soy sauce mixture, cornstarch mixture, onions, garlic, and meat. Stir fry for 2 or 3 minutes until mixture is hot. Stir in sesame oil, if used; sprinkle with peanuts. Serve with rice.

Note: If fresh ginger root is not available, use preserved or candied ginger, well washed.

Captain Ebanks' Fish Stew

This is an honest and delicious meal that was served to my family and me on a sailboat in the Cayman Islands. We were on vacation and had caught the ingredients ourselves spearfishing. But we didn't know what to do with them. Our captain, 23-year-old Ronald Ebanks, did, and his recipe is proof that it doesn't always take centuries of experience to be a good cook; Ronald seems to have been born with the knack. Give the recipe a try the next time you catch some fish—or the next time you head for the food store.

Makes 4 servings

> 1 large onion, sliced
> 4 tablespoons butter
> 1 cup ketchup
> 2 tablespoons fresh lime juice
> 2 teaspoons bottled steak sauce
> Dash of worcestershire sauce
> ½ teaspoon salt
> ⅛ teaspoon pepper
> 1½–2 pounds fresh fish fillets (red snapper, bass, or cod) or 2 packages (12 ounces each) frozen cod or fillet of sole

1. Sauté onion in butter for 5 minutes, or until soft, in a large, heavy skillet or Dutch oven. Add ketchup, lime juice, steak sauce, worcestershire sauce,

salt, and pepper. Bring to boiling.

2. Cut fish into serving-size pieces. Arrange in sauce, cover, and simmer for 20 minutes, or until fish flakes easily.

Mrs. Oscar McCollum's Southern Fried Chicken

Mrs. Oscar McCollum of Reidsville, North Carolina, said that all she ever wanted as a little girl, was "to grow up, get married, and have a lot of children so I could cook for them." And that's exactly what happened, as Jean Anderson, who interviewed Mrs. McCollum, reported in a recent Family Circle *article on grass roots cooking.*

Mrs. McCollum loves to cook— except on Sundays, when she puts her feet up and watches TV. Many of her recipes have won blue ribbons at county fairs, not to mention a lot of praise from her family.

Here are two of her favorite recipes that I especially enjoy. The southern fried chicken, Mrs. McCollum says, "is real crispy and brown outside and juicy all the way to the bone." And the pork sausage and tomato pies are good "because the juice from the tomatoes kind of drips down into the sausage meat." Try the recipes and see if you don't agree that she has really earned her blue ribbons.

Makes 4 servings

---

1 frying chicken (approximately 3 pounds), cut up
2 teaspoons salt (approximately)
¼ teaspoon pepper (approximately)
½ cup unsifted all-purpose flour
Lard for frying or, if you prefer, vegetable oil or shortening
1 tablespoon water
Chicken Gravy (recipe follows)

1. Lay chicken pieces in a shallow baking dish or pan, sprinkle with salt, cover, and refrigerate overnight. Next day, pour off all accumulated juices and pat chicken dry on paper toweling. Sprinkle chicken well with pepper, then roll in flour to coat, shaking off excess.
2. Melt enough lard or oil in a large, iron skillet over moderate heat to measure about 1 inch deep. Continue to heat. ("When it's frying temperature," says Mrs. McCollum, "you'll begin to see a little steam rising up.") Lay in pieces of chicken (it doesn't matter which side first) and adjust heat so chicken doesn't brown too fast (heat should be just moderate or moderately low).

3. Cook chicken for 30 minutes on one side, then turn and cook 30 minutes longer. Add water, cover, and let stand just until the fat stops sputtering.
4. Lay chicken pieces out on paper toweling to drain. Lay paper towels on top while preparing gravy. ("If the chicken's to be good and crispy, you don't want it to sweat," explains Mrs. McCollum.) Serve the fried chicken hot or cold.

Chicken Gravy

Makes about 2 cups

4 tablespoons drippings from skillet used to fry chicken
¼ cup unsifted all-purpose flour
2 cups water
½ teaspoon salt
⅛ teaspoon pepper

1. Pour all drippings from skillet, measure 4 tablespoons, and return to skillet. Add flour; heat and stir until flour turns brown.
2. Add water, salt, and pepper. Heat and stir slowly for about 5 minutes, until gravy thickens and there is no raw flour taste.
3. Pour into a gravy boat and serve with fresh-baked biscuits.

Mrs. Oscar McCollum's Pork Sausage and Tomato Pies

Makes 6 individual-size pies

1 recipe Short and Tender Piecrust (recipe follows)
¾ pound bulk sausage meat
2 small juicy-ripe tomatoes, sliced ½-inch thick

1. Prepare piecrust and divide in half; set aside while browning the sausage.
2. Shape sausage into cakes about 2½ inches across and ½-inch thick. If using a roll of sausage meat, simply slice it ½-inch thick. Fry sausage in a heavy skillet over moderate heat for 10 to 12 minutes, turning cakes or slices after 5 or 6 minutes so that both sides are lightly browned. Lift with a slotted spoon. Drain well on paper toweling.
3. Roll out piecrust, half at a time, on a lightly floured cloth to a thickness of about ⅛ inch. Cut into circles using about a 6-inch saucer as a pattern. Transfer pastry circles to a baking sheet and moisten the rims of each with a little water. Place a

sausage cake in the middle of each circle, then gather edges of pastry up over sausage and pinch together, leaving a small hole in the center so that the sausage cake shows.

4. Bake in a very hot oven, 450 degrees, for about 15 minutes, until it just begins to brown. Place a tomato slice in the center of each pie and bake about 15 minutes longer, or until nicely browned and bubbling. Serve hot.

VARIATION: PORK SAUSAGE AND TOMATO PIELETS

Makes 20 pielets

1. Prepare piecrust as directed.
2. Place sausage meat in a large, heavy skillet; break up with a fork and fry over moderately low heat for about 10 minutes, continuing to break up, just until the pink color has disappeared. Drain on paper toweling.
3. Roll out the piecrust, half at a time, into a 12-inch square; then divide into 4-inch squares. Transfer pastry squares to 2

baking sheets and moisten each corner of each pastry square with a little cold water.

4. Spoon about 1 tablespoon of sausage meat into the center of each square. Bring opposite corners up on top and pinch to seal to form little "bandana-like" bundles.
5. Bake in a very hot oven, 450 degrees, for 12–15 minutes, until pie begins to brown. Place half a cherry tomato, cut-side down, in the center of each pie. Bake 10 to 12 minutes longer until bubbly and browned. Serve hot as appetizers.

Short and Tender Piecrust

Makes enough for 1 9- or 10-inch double-crust pie

2 cups sifted all-purpose flour
¼ teaspoon salt
½ cup lard
⅓–½ cup cold water

1. Place flour and salt in a large shallow mixing bowl. Add lard and cut in with a pastry blender until crumbly, about the texture of uncooked oatmeal.
2. Add water, a few drops at a time, tossing briskly with a fork. The minute the mixture holds together, stop adding water.
3. Roll out pastry, ½ at a time, on a lightly floured pastry cloth, to desired size and shape.

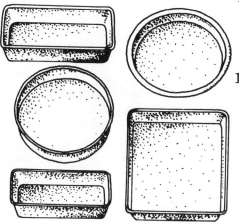

Canadian Pork Pie

Made with chopped pork and veal, onion, and lots of seasoning, this pie is a flavorful choice for a buffet table. It's also easy to make; the pies can be made ahead of time and frozen. When you're trying to pull together a complete company menu, this is a big help. Besides, I love this dish, so even if Nika Hazelton hadn't made it so simple to prepare, I'd still want to serve it.

Makes 2 8-inch pies

1 pound lean boneless pork
1 pound boneless veal
1 medium onion, chopped
1 clove garlic, minced
1 teaspoon salt
¼ teaspoon ground nutmeg
⅛ teaspoon mace
⅛ teaspoon cayenne
1 cup water
Pastry for 2 8-inch double-crust pies (2 packages piecrust mix)

1. Chop meats very finely with a sharp knife. (Do not grind them as grinding affects the flavor.) Place meats in a saucepan with onion, garlic, salt, nutmeg, mace, cayenne, and water; cover. Simmer, stirring frequently, for about 1 hour, or until meats are tender. When cooked, the mixture should be thick. Cool.

2. Prepare piecrust mix according to package directions. Line 2 8-inch pie plates with the pastry; spoon meat mixture into pastry-lined plates. Cover with top crusts; flute edges. Cut slits in top crusts to let steam escape.
3. Bake in a hot oven, 425 degrees, for 10 minutes. Lower oven temperature to moderate, 350 degrees, and bake for 40 to 45 minutes longer, or until pastry is golden-brown. Serve hot with chili sauce.

Note: Baked pies may be frozen and reheated in a moderate oven, 350 degrees, for about 30 minutes.

Florence Lin's Stir-Fried Pork with Peppers

One of the things I like about many Oriental dishes is that they're fairly quick to prepare. This particularly appeals to me when I feel like being a little creative in the kitchen, but don't want to stay there all day. This recipe is perfect for such moments. It was given to me by Florence Lin who runs a well-known cooking school in New York and who knows how to save not only time, but money, as you can see by the list of inexpensive ingredients called for in the recipe.

Makes 6 servings

3–4 ½-inch thick, hip pork chops, or 3 ½-inch thick shoulder pork chops, bone and fat removed, or 1 pound boneless pork cutlets
1½ teaspoons cornstarch
½ teaspoon sugar
2 tablespoons soy sauce
1 tablespoon water
5 tablespoons peanut or corn oil
6 cups 1-inch squares sweet green pepper (about 6 large peppers; see Note)

1½ teaspoons salt
 ½ teaspoon sugar
  1 tablespoon dry sherry
 ½ tablespoon cornstarch
  3 tablespoons water

1. Slice pork into pieces 2-by-½-by-⅛ inches. (There should be about 1½ cups.)
2. Combine cornstarch, sugar, soy sauce, and water in a medium-size bowl for the marinade. Add the pork, mixing well by hand. Reserve.
3. Heat a large skillet or wok until very hot. Add 2 tablespoons oil. Stir fry the peppers for 4 to 5 minutes. Add salt and sugar. Mix well and transfer to a warm platter.
4. Clean out the skillet; reheat until hot. Add remaining oil. Mix pork and marinade again and add to oil. Stir fry over high heat until pork begins to separate into slices and the color of all the meat has changed. Sprinkle in sherry. Add peppers; stir and cook to heat through.
5. Mix cornstarch with water and slowly pour into the skillet. Stir until sauce thickens and a clear glaze coats the meat and vegetables. Serve immediately.

Note: Cut-up zucchini, celery, asparagus, cauliflower, broccoli, green beans, cabbage, or a combination of mushrooms with one of the vegetables may be used instead of the green pepper. If vegetable needs more cooking after stir frying, add a tablespoon or two of water, cover and cook over high heat a few minutes longer. Do not overcook. Sliced beef or chicken can be substituted for the pork.

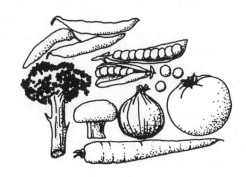

Horikawa's Sukiyaki

A few years ago James Trager wrote a marvelous story for Family Circle *on Japanese dishes to make at home. And while he didn't trot off to Japan for the recipes, Jim did do the next best thing—he interviewed Ryoji Yoshida, the chief chef at the famous Horikawa Restaurant in Los Angeles.*

Since Japanese food is one of my favorites, I've included two of chef Yoshida's recipes here: sukiyaki and tempura. To the uninitiated, tempura is a deep-fried seafood and vegetable dish, and sukiyaki, a one-pot beef (or chicken) and vegetable dish you can make right at the table. Both are just great.

Makes 4 servings

1–1½ pounds boneless lean tenderloin or sirloin steak
  1 10-ounce package fresh spinach, or 2 cups shredded Chinese cabbage, or 1 bunch watercress, or 1 cup sliced celery
  1 bunch green onions, trimmed and cut into 3-inch pieces
  1 large onion, cut into ½-inch slices and rings separated
4–6 mushrooms, cut into ¼-inch slices
  2 cakes soybean curd (tofu), cut into 1-inch cubes
  1 can (4 ounces) thread noodles (harusame)
  1 can (8 ounces) bamboo shoots
  ½ cup Japanese soy sauce
  ½ cup mirin (sweet sake) or dry sherry
  ⅓ cup sugar
  ½ teaspoon monosodium glutamate

PREPARE IN ADVANCE (UP TO 6 HOURS AHEAD OF TIME)

1. Trim any fat from steak and reserve. Place steak in freezer for 30 minutes, or until stiff enough to slice easily. Cut against the grain into ⅛-inch thick slices; halve the long slices.
2. Wash and drain spinach well; remove stems and break into small pieces.
3. If harusame are available, bring 1 cup water to a boil. Drop in the harusame, return to the boil, then drain and cut noodles into thirds.
4. If bamboo shoots are available, pare and cut in half, lengthwise. Cut into thin slices, crosswise, and wash under running water; drain.
5. Arrange beef, vegetables, and harusame in neat rows on a large platter. Cover platter with plastic wrap and refrigerate until serving time.

AT THE TABLE FOR EACH
SERVING

1. Place a large skillet over a table
   burner and preheat for several
   minutes, or preheat an electric
   skillet to the highest setting,
   400 to 425 degrees.
2. Rub part of the reserved fat
   over bottom of the hot skillet.
3. Place ¼ of the beef in the
   skillet; pour in 2 tablespoons
   soy sauce and sprinkle meat
   with 1 tablespoon sugar. Cook
   for a minute, stirring and turning, then push to one side.
4. Add ¼ of the vegetables (and
   tofu, harusame, and bamboo
   shoots, if available); sprinkle
   with 2 tablespoons sake or dry
   sherry and monosodium glutamate. Cook, stirring often, 4 to
   5 minutes longer, or until vegetables are crisply tender. (If
   food begins to stick or burn,
   lower heat and add a drop or
   two of cold water to the skillet.)
5. Quickly stir beef and vegetables
   together. Serve hot, while continuing to cook other portions.

Horikawa's Tempura

Makes 4 servings

Tempura Batter (recipe follows)
12–16 medium fresh or frozen
shrimp or 1 pound sea scallops, smelts, or fish fillets
¼ cup flour
1 large sweet potato
1 small acorn squash
1 large green pepper
1 large yellow onion
6 large mushrooms
2 large carrots
Oil (sesame 90%, vegetable
10%)
Dipping Sauce (recipe follows)

1. Prepare tempura batter and
   chill for at least 2 hours.
2. Shell and devein fresh shrimp
   or thaw frozen shrimp, following package directions; or cut
   fish into bite-size pieces. Dip
   fish, one piece at a time, into
   flour, shaking vigorously to remove excess flour.
3. Pare sweet potato and cut into
   ¼-inch slices. Halve acorn
   squash; seed and cut into ¼-
   inch strips and pare. Halve and
   seed pepper; cut into 1-inch

pieces. Cut onion into 1-inch slices and separate into rings. Cut mushrooms into ¼-inch slices. Scrape carrots and cut into ¼-inch diagonal slices.

4. Pour sesame and vegetable oils into a 10-inch skillet, deep-fat fryer, or electric skillet to a depth of 3 inches. Heat to 375 degrees on a deep-fat thermometer, or until a dab of batter dropped into the oil crisps and browns quickly.

5. Dip shrimp and vegetables in batter and then fry, no more than 6 to 8 pieces at a time, in the hot oil until food rises to the surface. Turn and fry until golden, about 1 minute. Remove with skimmer or slotted spoon to a cookie sheet lined with paper toweling. Keep hot in a very, very slow oven, 250 degrees.

6. Skim the surface of the oil to remove any excess pieces of batter; check temperature. Fry remaining food, about 6 pieces at a time.

7. Give each diner an individual bowl of dipping sauce. Serve tempura hot, either on individual plates or on a platter from which each diner will serve himself. Garnish platter with pieces of green onion, if you wish.

Tempura Batter

Makes about 3 cups, or enough batter to coat food for 4 servings

1 egg yolk
1 cup ice water
¾ cup sifted all-purpose flour

1. Combine egg yolk and ice water in a large bowl; sift in flour and mix lightly. (Batter should have consistency of pancake batter; thin enough to run off a spoon easily.)

2. Chill at least 2 hours. If too thick, thin with a few drops of cold water.

Dipping Sauce

Makes about 1½ cups

⅓ cup Japanese soy sauce
⅓ cup mirin (sweet sake) or sweet white wine
¼ teaspoon monosodium glutamate
1 cup water

1. Combine soy sauce, mirin or sweet wine, monosodium glutamate, and water.

2. Pour into 4 individual dipping bowls. Serve with tempura.

Grace Chu's Shrimp Chop Suey

"If you go to China," says cooking teacher *Madame Grace Zia Chu, "don't order chop suey."* It's a very popular but un-Chinese dish that was first created over one hundred years ago in California by Chinese immigrants, using whatever inexpensive ingredients they could find.

While Madame Chu usually teaches her students to make authentic Chinese dishes, she also shows them how to cook chop suey, and other Chinese-American specialties because they are a real part of our own heritage. To make matters really simple, Madame Chu says that if you don't have a wok for this recipe, it's perfectly acceptable to use a skillet or large saucepan. Now there's a practical woman!

Makes 6 servings

1 1-pound package frozen, shelled, de-veined shrimp
2 tablespoons vegetable oil
1 tablespoon dry sherry
½ teaspoon salt
1 cup shredded Chinese cabbage or spinach
½ cup fresh mushrooms, shredded
½ cup sliced celery
½ cup sliced onion
1 cup canned bean sprouts or ½ pound fresh bean sprouts
1 tablespoon cornstarch
½ cup chicken broth
1 tablespoon dark soy sauce
½ teaspoon sugar
¼ teaspoon monosodium glutamate (optional)

1. Split shrimp in half. Wash and drain.
2. Heat 1 tablespoon oil in a skillet. When it is hot, add shrimp. Stir fry for 1 minute. Add sherry and salt; cook for 1 minute. Remove and keep warm.
3. Heat remaining 1 tablespoon oil in skillet. Add cabbage (or spinach); mix quickly and cook for 1 minute. Add mushrooms, celery, and onion. Mix and cook for 2 minutes. Add drained bean sprouts. Mix well.
4. Mix cornstarch with broth, soy sauce, sugar, and monosodium glutamate in a small bowl; add to skillet. Cook for 2 minutes, or until thickened and bubbly. Add shrimp mixture; heat 1 minute more. Serve immediately.

Madame Chu's Orange Leek Duck

By her peers, she's considered an unrivaled authority on Chinese cooking; but Madame Grace Zia Chu is also considered an expert teacher by the more than 2,000 people who have studied with her over the years.

I also enjoy her recipes and find that many of them are quite easy. This orange leek duck, for instance, is considered a very special dish in China and one that's served mainly at banquets; but it doesn't require inordinate or hard-to-find ingredients or difficult preparation. It's served with orange slices, but the basting sauce is different from most duckling a l'orange recipes. And if prepared correctly, the duck should be tender enough that only a fork or chopsticks are needed to separate the meat from the bones.

Makes 4 servings

---

  1 frozen duckling (approximately 4 pounds), thawed
  1 teaspoon salt
  2 oranges
4½ cups water
  2 cups leek, cut into 2-inch pieces
  ¼ cup soy sauce
  ½ cup dry sherry
  2 tablespoons dark corn syrup

1. Remove giblets from duck and use for making broth. Sprinkle with salt.
2. Remove peel from oranges with a sharp knife in one continuous spiral, cutting through and removing white part and membrane around orange meat; reserve. Cut oranges in half; slice into ¼-inch slices.
3. Place duck on rack in roasting pan. Add 2 cups water to pan to catch drippings and prevent oven from smoking.
4. Roast duck in moderate oven, 350 degrees, for 1 hour. Before removing from oven, pierce skin with tines of fork to let fat run out.
5. Combine leek, soy sauce, and sherry in a Dutch oven or large kettle. Place duck on top, breast-side up. Bring to boiling. Add remaining 2½ cups water; bring to boiling again. Lower heat; cover. Simmer for 30 minutes, basting occasionally, then simmer for 30 minutes longer.
6. Roll up orange peel spirals; stuff into cavity. Pour corn syrup over duck. Continue cooking for 1 hour more, basting once with pan juices.
7. Remove cover; simmer for 10 minutes.

8. Place duck on platter. Arrange orange slices around and over it. Keep warm. Simmer juices remaining in Dutch oven until thickened. Pour over duck.

"21" Club Duckling Bigarade

One of the most satisfying meals I've ever had was duckling bigarade at "21." Here's their recipe for this extraordinary dish, obtained from reporters Susanna and Jason Berger.

Makes 4 servings

1 frozen duckling (approximately 5 pounds), thawed
1 teaspoon salt
¾ cup chopped celery
¾ cup chopped carrots
1 medium onion, chopped (½ cup)
2 bay leaves
1 tablespoon all-purpose flour
2 cups Quick Brown Sauce (recipe follows)
¼ cup madeira wine
½ cup currant jelly
1 cup sugar
½ cup white vinegar
1 California orange
½ cup dry sherry

1. Tie legs of duckling together with string. Sprinkle salt into small roasting pan (this prevents duckling from sticking to pan). Place duckling, breast side up, on top of salt.
2. Roast in hot oven, 400 degrees, for 1 hour and 15 minutes; pour off fat from roasting pan. Place chopped vegetables and bay leaves around duckling; mix with drippings. Roast for 15 minutes longer. Transfer duckling to a heated platter; keep warm while making sauce.
3. Turn vegetables and drippings into a medium-size saucepan. Skim off fat. Sprinkle flour over vegetables and stir in over medium heat. Add quick brown sauce and madeira; cover. Simmer, stirring often, for 10 minutes. Strain.
4. Combine currant jelly, ½ cup sugar, and vinegar in a medium-size saucepan. Cook over medium heat, stirring often,

until mixture is thickened and syrupy (caramelized), about 10 minutes. Add to quick brown sauce mixture; cover. Simmer, stirring often, for 30 minutes.

5. Peel the thin, bright orange zest from the orange with a vegetable parer. Cut zest into strips, ⅛ inch wide and 1½ inches long. Simmer strips in water to cover for 3 minutes; drain. Combine with remaining ½ cup sugar and sherry in a small saucepan. Cook until orange strips are transparent and syrup is slightly thickened, 10 to 15 minutes. Stir into quick brown sauce mixture (this is the bigarade sauce).

6. To serve duckling, arrange on platter with watercress. Spoon some of the sauce over duckling and cut reserved, peeled orange into slices to garnish duckling. Serve remaining sauce in a gravy boat.

Quick Brown Sauce

Makes 2 cups

3 tablespoons butter
¼ cup all-purpose flour
1 10½-ounce can condensed beef broth
⅔ cup water

1. Melt butter in a small saucepan; stir in flour. Cook, stirring constantly, over low heat, until mixture turns golden brown. Remove from heat.

2. Slowly stir in broth and water. Continue cooking and stirring until the sauce thickens and bubbles for 1 minute. Lower heat; simmer for 5 minutes.

Lena Erculiani's Chicken Cacciatora

Gallitzin, Pennsylvania, may seem an unlikely place to go for authentic Italian food. Nonetheless, that's what you'll find at the Erculiani Restaurant there. Owned and run by the Erculiani family, the restaurant serves some unique versions of popular Italian dishes, such as this one devised by chief chef Lena Erculiani. I think you'll want to add it to your own recipe collection.

Makes 8 servings

2 broiler–fryer chickens (2½ pounds each), cut up
½ cup flour
1½ teaspoons salt
1 teaspoon pepper
½ cup vegetable oil
1 tablespoon plus 1 teaspoon leaf rosemary, crumbled
½ cup dry sherry
Sauce (recipe follows)

1. Shake chicken in plastic bag with flour, 1 teaspoon salt, and ½ teaspoon pepper. Heat oil in large skillet (use 2 skillets if necessary), and add 1 tablespoon rosemary. Brown chicken slowly, but thoroughly, on both sides in oil.
2. Remove chicken to a shallow pan. Bake in moderate oven, 350 degrees, for 15 minutes, or until tender. Remove from oven. Pour off any excess oil; sprinkle sherry over chicken. Let stand while preparing sauce.
3. Add chicken and any wine remaining in pan to the sauce. Season with ½ teaspoon salt, ½ teaspoon pepper, 1 teaspoon rosemary. Simmer, covered, for 5 minutes; taste and add more seasoning, if needed. Serve with hot cooked noodles or rice.

Sauce

Makes about 5½ cups

4 tablespoons (½ stick) butter
1 cup chopped onion
½ cup chopped celery
½ pound mushrooms, sliced
1 can (13¾ ounces) chicken broth
1 can (1 pound) Italian plum tomatoes, drained
½ cup grated parmesan cheese

1. Heat butter in a large saucepan or Dutch oven. Sauté onion and celery for about 5 minutes. Add mushrooms; sauté for 5 minutes longer.
2. Add 1 cup broth; bring to boiling. Lower heat; simmer until vegetables are tender and liquid is almost evaporated.
3. Stir in the remaining broth, tomatoes, and cheese. Cook until slightly thickened, 3 to 4 minutes.

Ann Seranne's Roast Prime Ribs of Beef

Ann Seranne has written numerous cookbooks, contributed to many magazines, and was the former food editor of the New York Post *and an executive editor of* Gourmet *magazine. I first met her when she helped us with a reader recipe contest at* Family Circle *and it was during this time that I grew to understand why she has a reputation as one of America's great food authorities. She not only knows how to judge whether a recipe will work, but she knows whether it's original or not.*

I think you'll enjoy the recipes she's given me for this book. They include this one, which Ann says is her favorite way of cooking a rib roast. One of the secrets behind her method, she notes, is in the special way it is roasted. Try it—it's juicier this way. Take the roast directly from the refrigerator and put it into a preheated, hot oven; roast it for the exact time, then turn the oven off and let the roast sit there for anywhere from one to three hours (without opening the oven door).

Each rib serves 2 people

1 rib roast of beef (2–5 ribs, without the short ribs)
Flour
Salt
Coarsely cracked pepper

1. Preheat oven to 500 degrees.
2. Remove roast from refrigerator and place in a shallow, open roasting pan. Sprinkle with a little flour and rub the flour into the fat. Season generously with salt and pepper.
3. Put roast in the preheated oven (be sure temperature has reached 500 degrees) and roast for 15 minutes per rib. (Or, 18 to 20 minutes per rib for medium to medium-well.) Set a timer so that the meat does not overcook. (To protect the oven from spattering fat, place a tent of aluminum foil lightly over the top.)
4. When cooking time is up, turn off oven heat. DO NOT OPEN OVEN DOOR. Let roast remain in the oven for at least 1 hour, or until oven is lukewarm.

Ann Seranne's Baked Lobster

"In my estimation, and many others' who have eaten baked lobster at my home, this is the very best way to cook a live lobster. The gentle heat of the oven cannot toughen the delicate flesh, nor dilute its flavor."

I was intrigued when Ann Seranne told me this because I'd never had baked lobster. Since receiving her recipe, I've found out how right she is—this is the best!

Fresh lobsters (1–1½ pounds each)
Salt
Coarsely cracked pepper
Butter
Lemon juice and lemon wedges

1. If you cannot kill live lobsters (I can't), ask the fish market to do it and pack them on a bed of crushed ice, to keep cool. Put them in the refrigerator and cook them as soon as possible.
2. Arrange the lobsters side by side, shell side down, in a baking pan. Fold the large claws in front of the eyes.
3. Sprinkle lightly with salt and generously with pepper. Arrange thin slices of butter on claws and down the tail. Sprinkle generously with lemon juice.

4. Bake in a preheated, moderate oven, 350 degrees, for 30 minutes, basting half way through the baking time, with juices in the pan.
5. Serve with additional melted butter and lemon wedges.

Ann's Roast Turkey with All the Trimmings

"If possible," says Ann Seranne, "use a fresh turkey for this recipe." And to make it perfect, cook it in a hot oven with lots of butter and loads of basting sauce. In addition to this advice, Ann clearly outlines how to go about making a delicious turkey, starting with some things you can do a day or two ahead of time. I particularly like the recipe because the stuffing includes fresh oysters and the gravy is rich and well seasoned.

Makes 8 to 12 servings

1 fresh tom turkey (12–14 pounds), ready to cook
1 large onion, chopped
2 cups chopped celery, including a few of the leaves
12 cups cubed bread (24 slices) or 1½ packages stuffing mix (8 ounces each)
2 teaspoons salt
1 teaspoon pepper
1 teaspoon poultry seasoning
1 teaspoon sage
1½ cups warm water or 1 pint freshly shucked oysters with liquor (optional)

PREPARE IN ADVANCE

1. Remove all fat from the body cavity of the turkey and sauté it in a large skillet until the fat is rendered and the bits of tissue are brown and crispy.

2. Add onion and celery; sauté for about 10 minutes, or until vegetables are tender but not brown. Combine vegetable mixture and fat with bread crumbs. Add the salt, pepper, poultry seasoning, and sage.

3. Moisten with warm water or stir in oysters along with their liquid. Mix lightly, cool, and then refrigerate until ready to stuff bird. (But do not make more than 4 hours ahead of time.)

STUFFING AND TRUSSING TURKEY

1. Scrape out any bits of blood and viscera left in the turkey and rinse it out with cold water. Dry well with paper towels.
2. Stuff the neck opening lightly with stuffing. Fold neck skin over back of turkey and fasten it to the back with a poultry skewer or "nail." Fold wing tips back under the bird.
3. Stuff body cavity lightly, allowing room for stuffing to expand. Insert skewers at intervals across the opening. Lace the opening with heavy string much as you would lace a boot, starting from the part nearest the breast bone and lacing down to the tail, leaving long ends of string hanging.
4. Turn turkey over and insert a poultry skewer through the base of the tail. Turn turkey breast side up again. Press legs close to body; tie ends of drumsticks together and fasten to the skewer.
5. Bring the two ends of string between the body and thighs on each side, then under the bird and up around the main joint of the wings. Finally run the strings under the wing tips at the back and tie across the back. (This method trusses the bird nicely and doesn't leave any string marks over the breast.) Bird is now ready to roast.

ROASTING TURKEY AND MAKING GRAVY

Makes about 5 cups gravy

½ pound (2 sticks) butter
½ cup boiling water
  Turkey giblets
½ teaspoon peppercorns
¼ teaspoon thyme
1 teaspoon salt
  Few sprigs parsley
1 stalk celery with leaves
1 small onion, coarsely cut
⅓ cup flour

1. Place trussed turkey, breast side up, in a shallow roasting pan. Spread the skin with butter. Add boiling water to the roasting pan and roast turkey in hot oven, 475 degrees, for 30 minutes. Reduce oven temperature to 350 degrees and continue to roast for about 3 hours, or until turkey is done, basting every half hour with the butter and juices in the roasting pan. When thighs and legs become a light mahogany color, cover them with a buttered piece of brown paper.
2. When turkey is in the oven, put the giblets, except the liver, into a 3-quart saucepan and cover generously with water.

Add peppercorns, thyme, salt, parsley, celery, and onion. Bring water to a boil and simmer for 2 hours, adding a little more water from time to time. Add turkey liver and simmer for 10 minutes longer. Strain broth into a clean saucepan. (There should be 1 quart turkey stock, so add water if necessary.) Chop liver and giblets, adding any little tender bits of meat pulled from the neck. Set aside.

3. Transfer turkey to a serving platter and return to the warm oven, heat off.

4. Pour off all but 3 tablespoons fat from roasting pan, taking care not to discard any of the meat juices. Place roasting pan over direct heat. Stir in ⅓ cup flour. Gradually stir in 1 quart turkey stock. Cook, stirring in all the crisp, brown bits of glaze from the bottom and sides of the pan to make a deep brown gravy. Add chopped giblets and boil for 5 minutes, stirring occasionally. Correct seasoning with salt and pepper. Pour into gravy boat.

Ann's Poached Chicken with Lemon Sauce

Patterned after the Greek chicken Avgolemono, *this delicate dish is really good when served with a rice pilaf and, of course, the delicious lemon sauce made with fresh lemon and egg yolks. It's Ann Seranne's recipe, and I wouldn't be without it.*

Makes 4 servings

1 frying chicken (3½ pounds), quartered
1 teaspoon salt
½ teaspoon peppercorns
1 clove garlic, halved
1 medium onion, peeled and coarsely sliced
3 stalks celery with leaves, coarsely cut
1 hot red pepper pod
1 bay leaf
½ teaspoon thyme
½ lemon, sliced
3 tablespoons butter
4 tablespoons flour
2 egg yolks
1 lemon, whole

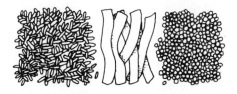

1. Put chicken into a heavy kettle and add water to barely cover. Add salt, peppercorns, garlic, onion, celery, red pepper, bay leaf, thyme, and sliced lemon.
2. Bring liquid to a boil, turn heat to very low. Partially cover and simmer for 45 minutes, or until chicken is tender. The liquid should not actively boil. There must be at least 3 cups broth.
3. Remove hot chicken from broth to a warm serving platter and cover with foil to keep moist and warm. Correct seasoning of broth with salt; strain enough into a bowl to measure 3 cups.
4. In a saucepan melt butter. Stir in flour and cook, stirring, until mixture bubbles. Remove from heat. Add the hot broth, return pan to heat, and stir rapidly until sauce is smooth and slightly thickened.
5. In a small bowl beat egg yolks with juice of the whole lemon and a little of the hot sauce. Stir into remaining sauce and cook, stirring, for 1 minute, without letting the sauce boil. Remove immediately from heat and pour over the chicken.

Note: If desired, 4 small carrots and 4 small onions may be cooked and served with the chicken and sauce.

Zesty Welsh Rabbit

I will risk sounding chauvinistic and say that beer is primarily a man's drink. Honestly, I've known very few women who enjoy it as much as men. But it was a woman who introduced me to cooking with beer and to the fact that this plebeian beverage takes on all kinds of interesting flavor changes when it's heated. The woman was Nika Hazelton and she demonstrated, by giving me this recipe and others, how beer can add a subtle flavor to familiar foods that's different enough to make them more interesting, but "not so different as to make traditionalists and children recoil with horror." Nika says you can use either lager, ale, or stout in this recipe, and that it doesn't matter whether it's fresh or stale beer. And of course, if you're a beer drinker, you'll want a glass of it with the rabbit as well as in it! I always do.

Makes 4 servings

- 2 cups sharp cheddar cheese (8 ounces), shredded
- 1 tablespoon flour
- ½ teaspoon dry mustard
- 1 tablespoon butter
- ⅛–¼ teaspoon Tabasco
- ¼ cup beer or ale
- 8 slices white bread

1. Combine cheese, flour, mustard, butter, and Tabasco in a medium-size saucepan. Gradually stir in beer (the mixture should be rather thick).
2. Cook cheese mixture over low heat, stirring constantly, until cheese is melted.
3. While rabbit heats, trim crusts from bread and cut each slice into 2 triangles.
4. Toast bread in the broiler on one side only. Pour the melted cheese over the toast; serve immediately.

Note: The cheese mixture may be prepared ahead of time and refrigerated for 1 to 2 days.

Helen McCully's Veal Cordon Bleu

Helen McCully may be considered one of the tsarinas among cooking editors, but she is very down to earth when it comes to good food. Food editor of House Beautiful *and author of several marvelous cookbooks, including* The Waste Not, Want Not Cookbook, *Helen is one of the truly great creative cooks in our business. And she concentrates on the kinds of food people love best.*

Makes 6 servings

- 12 veal scallops from the leg (3–4 ounces each)
  - Salt
  - Pepper
- 6 thin, round slices prosciutto
- 6 thin slices gruyère or Switzerland swiss cheese
- 2 eggs, lightly beaten with 1 teaspoon water
  - All-purpose flour
- 1½ cups fresh bread crumbs (approximately 3 slices bread)
- 8 tablespoons (1 stick) unsalted butter, cut up

1. Place each scallop between two pieces of wax paper and pound with a mallet until very thin. Sprinkle each piece lightly with salt and pepper. Top each scallop with a slice of prosciutto and a slice of cheese.
2. With a pastry brush, coat the outside edges of each scallop with the beaten egg mixture. Top with another slice of the veal. Sprinkle some flour on a piece of wax paper and coat the scallops on both sides, shaking off any excess.
3. Dip scallops in the beaten eggs; coat well with the bread crumbs. Pat scallops with a heavy kitchen knife to help the bread crumbs stick. Carefully lift the meat to a cake rack and refrigerate for at least 2 hours. (This also helps the breading adhere to the meat.)
4. To cook, heat butter in a large, heavy skillet. When hot, but not smoking, sauté the cutlets until golden on both sides. Arrange on a heated serving platter and garnish with parsley sprigs.

Helen McCully's Coq au Vin

Makes 6 to 8 servings

¼ pound salt pork or unsmoked bacon all in one piece
9 tablespoons (1 stick plus 1 tablespoon) butter
2 ready-to-cook broiler–fryer chickens (each about 2½–3 pounds), cut up for frying
Salt
Pepper
¼ cup cognac or brandy
1 bottle (26 ounces) dry white wine
2 cans (10½ ounces each) condensed chicken broth
2 cloves garlic, peeled and crushed
4 bay leaves
½ teaspoon dried thyme
4 tablespoons peanut or vegetable oil
36 small white onions, peeled
½ pound button mushrooms, very thinly sliced
3 tablespoons all-purpose flour

1. Cut the rind off the salt pork; cut into 1-by-¼-inch pieces. Place in a heavy saucepan with enough water to cover. Bring to a boil; simmer for 10 minutes. Drain and rinse in cold water. Dry with paper towels.
2. Heat 2 tablespoons butter in a heavy skillet; add pork pieces

and fry slowly until lightly browned. Lift from the fat to paper towels. Set aside.

3. Pat the pieces of chicken dry with paper towels. Brown on both sides in hot fat. Sprinkle with salt and pepper.

4. Combine the pork and chicken pieces in a large heatproof casserole that can go to the table. Heat the cognac in a small saucepan, ignite, and pour over chicken. Shake casserole until the flames die out.

5. Add wine and enough of the chicken broth so the chicken pieces are completely covered. Add garlic, bay leaves, and thyme. Bring to a boil. Reduce heat to simmer; cover and cook slowly for 25 to 30 minutes, or until the chicken is tender when pierced with a fork and juices run clear. Lift chicken from the casserole and set both aside.

6. Heat 3 tablespoons butter with 3 tablespoons peanut oil in a large, heavy skillet. When hot, add onions and sauté over medium heat for about 10 minutes, or just long enough to brown the onions. (They will not brown evenly all over.) Shake the pan as they cook to keep the onions turning over. Add the remaining chicken broth. Cover; simmer

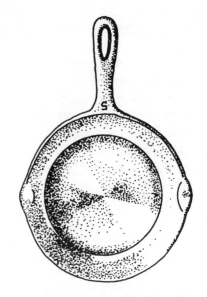

until onions are tender, about 20 minutes. Set aside.

7. Heat 2 tablespoons butter with the remaining oil in a second large skillet. As soon as the fat is very hot, add mushrooms. Toss and shake the pan for 4 to 5 minutes. As soon as they have browned lightly, remove from heat and set aside.

8. Place the casserole back on the fire. Bring to a rolling boil and continue to boil until there are about 3 cups liquid left. Lift out and discard the bay leaves and skim off any superfluous fat with a metal spoon.

9. Mix all remaining butter with flour to make a beurre manie. Drop by bits into the simmering liquid and cook, whipping constantly with a wire whip, for 2 to 3 minutes, or until the

sauce has thickened sufficiently to coat a spoon. Add the chicken pieces, onions, and mushrooms. Bring to a boil. Correct seasoning. (The coq au vin can be prepared in advance to this point and reheated later.)

10. To finish the dish (or reheat it), place over medium heat and slowly bring to a boil. Reduce heat and simmer just long enough to heat the chicken through. Do not cook further or chicken will become tough and stringy. Serve straight from the casserole, garnished with a bouquet of fresh parsley accompanied by freshly boiled potatoes and a nice big, green salad vinaigrette.

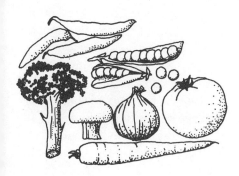

Perla Meyers' Cassoulet

In the last few years cassoulet has emerged from its humble status as a French peasant dish to become one of the most popular French dishes on both sides of the Atlantic. Probably some of the credit is due to fantastic cooks like Perla Meyers who, in my opinion, represent the new breed of French cooks—cooks who bring a down-to-earth approach to a food that has classically been regarded as difficult to make. Perla, aside from being young and beautiful, is the much admired author of the award-winning The Seasonal Kitchen *and* The Peasant Kitchen.

Perla notes that this recipe is time consuming, but is a practical one for company because it's a meal all by itself. And while she usually makes cassoulet from leftovers, her recipe shows how to start from scratch, since most people don't plan the weekly menu to include the assortment of meats called for in the recipe. But either way, you'll find it a really hearty, good dish.

Makes 8 to 12 servings

2 pounds dried white beans (preferably Great Northern)
1 pound unsliced bacon
10–11 cups light chicken bouillon or stock
1 pound garlic sausage
3 medium onions, peeled
1 bud garlic, unpeeled (the whole garlic)
4 sprigs parsley
2 bay leaves
1 celery stalk with leaves, coarsely chopped
½ teaspoon leaf thyme
6 peppercorns
1 teaspoon salt
Roast Duck (recipe follows)
The Meats (recipe follows)
4 tablespoons duck fat
1 cup plain, dry bread crumbs
½ cup minced parsley
3 cloves garlic, minced

1. Pick over beans and wash in cold running water; place in a large glass or ceramic bowl and cover with cold water. Cover bowl; soak overnight.
2. Blanch bacon slab in boiling water for 5 minutes; remove and drain on paper towels. Cut into ¼-inch slices and reserve.
3. The next day, drain beans and cover with chicken bouillon in a 4-quart heatproof casserole. Add sausage, bacon, and onions. Tie a bouquet of garlic, parsley, bay leaves, celery, thyme, and peppercorns in cheesecloth; add to casserole with salt. Bring to boiling on surface burner; cover casserole.
4. Bake in slow oven, 325 degrees, for 1 hour. Remove sausage and cut into thin slices; reserve. Continue baking beans for 45 minutes longer, or until beans are tender, but not falling apart. Discard bouquet and onions; strain beans and reserve all cooking liquid. (If you are not going to assemble cassoulet at this time, keep them in the cooking liquid, until ready to prepare dish.)
5. Spoon a thick layer of beans into the bottom of 4-quart heat-proof casserole. Top with a layer of roast duck, the meats, garlic sausage slices, and bacon slices. Continue layering casserole, ending with beans, reserving 6 slices garlic sausage for the top.
6. Pour reserved cooking liquids into casserole until it almost reaches the top of beans; reserve remaining liquid.
7. Heat duck fat in a small skillet; add bread crumbs, parsley, and minced garlic. Cook for 2 minutes, stirring constantly. Spoon mixture over beans and top with reserved garlic sausage.
8. Heat casserole on top of stove until juices begin to bubble;

cover loosely with aluminum foil.

9. Bake in moderate oven, 350 degrees, for 1½ hours; uncover. Add more reserved cooking liquids to casserole, if needed. Bake for 30 minutes longer, or until topping is crisp and nicely browned. Serve as soon as possible with a well-seasoned green salad and a full-bodied red wine.

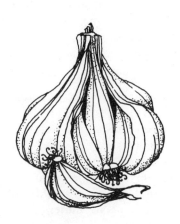

Roast Duck

1 frozen duckling (4 to 5 pounds), thawed
Salt
Pepper
1 large onion, peeled and halved
2 cups chicken bouillon or stock

1. Wipe duckling well with paper towels. Trim excess fat from duckling. Prick all over with a two-tined fork; season with salt and pepper. Place in a large baking pan with onion halves.

2. Roast in moderate oven, 350 degrees, for 2½ hours, basting with chicken bouillon, turning duckling two or three times, and removing fat as it accumulates. Reserve fat as it is removed from the pan.

3. Remove duckling from baking pan; cool until it is easy to handle. Slip meat from the bones.

The Meats

1 pound pork butt, cubed
1 pound lamb shoulder, cubed
Salt
Pepper
2–3 tablespoons duck fat or butter
4 medium onions, finely minced (2 cups)
2 large cloves garlic, finely minced
1 can (2 pounds 3 ounces) Italian plum tomatoes, well drained
2 teaspoons tomato paste
1 cup dry white wine
1 sprig parsley
1 bay leaf
¼ teaspoon leaf thyme
3–4 cups beef bouillon

1. Season pork and lamb cubes with salt and pepper. Brown, a few pieces at a time, in a large heavy heatproof casserole in duck fat or butter. Remove and reserve.
2. Pour off all but 2 tablespoons pan drippings; sauté onion and garlic until golden brown.
3. Add tomatoes, tomato paste, wine, salt, and pepper. Bring to boiling and boil until mixture is reduced by ⅓. Return meats to casserole. Tie a bouquet of parsley, bay leaf, and thyme in cheesecloth. Add to casserole with enough beef bouillon to cover meat by 1 inch. Cover casserole and place in center of oven. (It can be baked along with the soaked beans.)
4. Bake in moderate oven, 350 degrees, for 1½ hours, or until meats are tender, but not falling apart. Remove from oven; allow to stand for 10 minutes. Skim fat from surface. Strain meats and set aside. Add pan liquid to bean cooking liquid and reserve.

Frogs' Legs Provençale with Tomatoes Concasser from La Grenouille

Although the entire staff at this beautiful restaurant knows how to prepare Frogs' Legs Provençale, this version of Chef Henri's is my first choice, particularly when served with a garnish of chopped sautéed tomatoes. The recipe for those is included here, too, thanks to the chef's generous spirit.

Makes 1–2 portions

12–16 pairs frogs' legs (according to size)
  ½ cup milk
    Salt
    Pepper
  ½ cup all-purpose flour
   3 tablespoons vegetable oil
   3 tablespoons butter
 2–3 cloves garlic, finely chopped
 1–2 tablespoons finely chopped parsley
    Tomatoes Concasser (recipe follows)

1. Dip frogs' legs, a few at a time, into milk in a glass pie plate; place on wax paper and season with salt and pepper.
2. Dredge seasoned frogs' legs in flour, lifting up legs and shaking off excess flour.

3. Heat oil in a large, heavy skillet; add frogs' legs and brown quickly on all sides. Add butter, garlic, and parsley. Cook quickly, shaking pan constantly until butter just begins to turn bubbly and then topaz color (be careful not to burn). (Chef Henri does not sauté the garlic separately, as he feels there is a danger of the garlic overcooking and becoming bitter. He adds it last for a few minutes, while making the beurre noir.)

4. Turn frog legs immediately onto a heated serving dish and place a spoonful of tomatoes concasser on the side.

Note: The classic cooking oil for this dish is olive oil, but at La Grenouille, they have found that the flavor of olive oil is too strong for the palates of their guests. The garniture, tomatoes concasser, is not classically served with frogs' legs in Provence, but is the distinctive touch of La Grenouille.

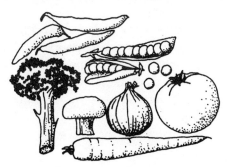

Tomatoes Concasser

Makes enough for 4 servings

4 large, ripe tomatoes
3 tablespoons vegetable oil
½ large onion, chopped (½ cup)
Salt
Pepper
1 clove garlic, finely chopped
½ bay leaf, crumbled
Dash of sugar

1. Dip tomatoes into boiling water for 15 seconds; then dip into a pan of cold water. Peel off skins. Scoop out the seeds by slicing off the blossom end and inserting a teaspoon. Coarsely chop tomatoes.

2. Heat oil in a flat-bottomed sauté pan; add onion and sauté for 7 to 8 minutes, or until very soft, but not brown.

3. Add chopped tomatoes, salt and pepper to taste, garlic, bay leaf, and a pinch of sugar (to compensate for the tomatoes' acidity).

4. Reduce heat to very low and simmer for 30 minutes (or until sauce has thickened and most of the liquid has evaporated), uncovered, shaking pan every so often.

Mefr's Oyster Stew à la "Souper Bowl"

Mefr (my wife—her name derives from her initials) serves this delicious dish, based on a traditional recipe, annually at our house during the half-time of the Super Bowl. Multiplied four times, it amply serves about 14 people, along with sea toast and oyster crackers with plenty of unsalted butter to spread on them. With a tall, frosty glass of beer, no one needs any supper that night!

Makes 3 or 4 servings

4 tablespoons (½ stick) salted butter
½ teaspoon celery salt (or to taste)
Dash of worcestershire sauce (to taste)
1 pint shelled oysters with liquor
¼ cup cold water
¼ pint heavy cream or light cream or half and half
1 pint milk (approximately)
Pepper
Salt (to taste)

1. Place all but 1 teaspoon butter, celery salt, and worcestershire sauce in pan (or top of double boiler) on low heat. Heat gently until butter melts.
2. While butter is melting, pour oysters and their liquor into a sieve placed over a bowl. Slowly pour water over oysters. Take oysters out of sieve one by one, and place in container, feeling each one carefully for bits of shell. Carefully scrape sieve to save every bit of liquor, and pour all of liquid over oysters. If oysters are unusually large, cut them in several pieces, or if preferred, keep them whole.
3. Pour oysters and the liquor-water combination into the pan with the melted butter combination.
4. Heat very gently, just until the edges of the oysters get curly. (Watch them very carefully as it doesn't take long—the edges will look slightly wavy when they're done.) Be sure not to overcook, as the oysters will get tough.
5. Add cream and milk and heat until warm. Add pepper.
6. Taste and add more milk or salt, if needed. (Celery salt is *not* very salty—you may need quite a bit more salt in order to bring out the flavor.)

7. When ready to serve, float remaining pat of butter on top, and garnish with chopped parsley or green onions.

Oyster Bar Fried Clams

For years the Oyster Bar in Grand Central Station was accepted as one of the seafood places in New York. Then, gradually, it seemed to go downhill, fall into disrepair, and eventually it closed. Most people were sad to see its demise, but accepted it in the spirit that, like the railroads themselves, it had seen its time.

Jerry Brody was willing to stake his reputation—and his money—to disprove this. He started by restoring the restaurant's decor, stripping away years of disinterest and neglect, and by then re-establishing the restaurant's original menu—complete with dozens of varieties of clams, oyster stew, and one of its most noted dishes and one I especially like, fried clams. Needless to say, Jerry succeeded and happily proved that people will seek out a good restaurant, whether it's off the beaten track or in the basement of a railroad station. Incidentally, if you're not used to good fried clams, these will be a welcome change. They're light, crispy, thinly breaded, and delicious.

Makes 4 servings

4 dozen soft clams, such as Ipswich or steamers
¼ cup all-purpose flour
1 egg
2 tablespoons milk
1½ cups unsalted soda cracker crumbs
Salt
Pepper
Shortening or vegetable oil for frying

1. Scrub clams with a stiff brush to remove sand. Open with a very heavy sharp knife or a clam opener; reserve clam liquid for another use.
2. Drain clams on paper towels. Coat lightly with flour on wax paper; shake off excess.
3. Beat egg with milk in a pie plate. Dip clams, one at a time, first into egg mixture, then into cracker crumbs seasoned with salt and pepper in a second pie plate. Shake off excess crumbs and place clams on paper towels until all are coated. Fry immediately.
4. Melt enough shortening or pour in enough oil to make a 2-inch depth in an electric deep-fat fryer or large heavy saucepan. Heat to 350 or 375 degrees, or until a cube of bread turns golden in 1 minute.

5. Fry clams, 3 or 4 at a time, for 3 minutes, or until golden. Remove with slotted spoon; drain on paper towels. Serve immediately with lemon wedges and tartar sauce or cocktail sauce, if you wish.

Marian Burros' Butterflied Leg of Lamb for the Outdoor Grill

Marian Burros is perhaps best known for her popular cookbook, Freeze with Ease. *But to readers of the* Washington Post, *she's also known as a first-rate food editor who not only reports on foods people like, but also the best and easiest ways to prepare them.*

I first met Marian years ago when she did a food feature for Family Circle *on Mrs. Mark Hatfield. Her article was excellent and so is this recipe she gave me for butterflied lamb, to be cooked on the outdoor grill.*

Makes 6 to 8 servings

1 6-pound leg of lamb, boned and butterflied
6–8 cloves garlic
1 cup salad or olive oil
2 teaspoons dried tarragon
2 tablespoons ground cumin seed
Salt
Pepper

1. Have the butcher bone the leg of lamb and butterfly it, if he will. Otherwise, simply slice thick portions so that the meat lies flat. Place lamb in roasting pan.
2. Crush garlic or put through press and sprinkle over lamb. Combine oil with half the tarragon and cumin and spoon over meat. Marinate at room temperature for 1 hour; turn meat and sprinkle with remaining tarragon and cumin. Baste and turn occasionally; continue marinating at room temperature for 2 hours more, or in the refrigerator overnight.
3. To cook, remove from marinade, season with salt and pepper, and grill over medium-hot coals 4 to 6 inches from heat for 45 minutes. Baste with marinade, turning occasionally. The meat should be pink on the inside and well done on the outside. Slice thinly to serve.

Diana Kennedy's Swiss Chard Enchiladas

More than any other writer, Diana Kennedy is responsible for giving Mexican cooking a whole new importance and stature among the world's cuisines. She has written two superb cookbooks on the subject, Cuisines of Mexico *and* The Tortilla Book. *Here's her recipe for a Mexican dish I especially enjoy.*

Makes 6 servings

2 pounds Swiss chard or 1 pound fresh spinach, well washed
6 tablespoons vegetable oil (approximately)
1 large clove garlic, peeled and finely chopped
1 teaspoon salt
¼ teaspoon pepper
3 medium tomatoes (about 1 pound 2 ounces) or 1 1-pound can tomatoes, drained (see Note)
1 small onion
1 clove garlic
2 hot chilies, fresh or canned, seeds removed
1 cup water
Salt
Vegetable oil
18 tortillas, frozen or canned
1 cup dairy sour cream
1 cup mild cheddar cheese, shredded
1 large onion, thinly sliced and separated into rings

1. Cook chard or spinach in small quantity of water, stirring occasionally, for about 5 minutes. Drain and chop coarsely. Heat 3 tablespoons oil in a large saucepan and cook the garlic without browning. Add chard or spinach and cook, stirring gently for about 3 minutes. Add salt and pepper; reserve.
2. Place tomatoes, onion, garlic, and chilies in an electric blender; whirl until smooth, but do not overblend. Heat 3 tablespoons oil; add the blender mixture and cook, stirring and scraping the bottom of the pan for 5 minutes. Add water and salt to taste; cook for 1 minute longer. Keep warm.
3. Heat ¼-inch of oil in a small skillet. Lower heat and fry tortillas, one by one, briefly on each side until heated through and limp. (They should never become crisp around the edges.) Drain on paper toweling.
4. Spread a rounded tablespoon of tomato sauce across the tortilla; add a little chard or spinach and sour cream. Roll loosely; place side by side in a warm 13-by-9-by-2-inch baking dish.
5. Reheat the remaining tomato sauce and pour over the enchiladas. Sprinkle with cheese and place under a preheated

broiler until cheese melts. Garnish with onion rings.

Note: If using fresh tomatoes, broil until skins blister; peel. If using canned tomatoes, use the juice as part of the 1 cup water called for.

Sheryl Julian's Gougère with Mushrooms and Ham

I only recently discovered this puff pastry masterpiece, and it was Sheryl Julian who introduced me to it. Sheryl is an avid cook and devotes much of her time to teaching cooking classes at Mount Vernon College and in her home in Washington, D.C. She also does catering, writes for the food section of the Washington Post, *and was the assistant editor of the prestigious 20-volume* Grand Diplome Cooking Course. *What more could you ask for in the way of expertise?*

Makes 6 servings

- 4 tablespoons butter
- 2 medium onions, chopped (1 cup)
- ½ pound mushrooms, sliced
- 1½ tablespoons flour
- 1 teaspoon salt
- ¼ teaspoon pepper
- 1 envelope or 1 teaspoon instant chicken broth
- 1 cup hot water
- 2 large tomatoes, peeled, quartered and seeded (2 cups)
- 6 ounces cooked ham, cut into thin strips (1½ cups)
  Pâte à Choux (recipe follows)
- 2 tablespoons shredded cheddar cheese
- 2 tablespoons chopped parsley

1. Melt butter in a large skillet. Sauté onion until soft, but not browned. Add mushrooms and continue cooking for 2 minutes.
2. Sprinkle with flour, salt, and pepper; mix and cook for 2 minutes longer. Add instant chicken broth and water; mix well. Bring to boiling, stirring constantly. Simmer for 4 minutes. Remove sauce from heat.
3. Cut each tomato quarter into 4 strips and add to the sauce with the ham strips. Taste; add additional seasoning, if needed.
4. Butter a 10- or 11-inch ovenproof skillet, pie plate, or shallow baking dish. Spoon the pâte à choux in a ring around

the edge, leaving the center open. Pour the filling into the center and sprinkle all over with cheese.

5. Bake in a hot oven, 400 degrees, for 40 minutes or until gougère is puffed and brown and the filling is bubbling. Sprinkle with parsley and serve at once, cut into wedges as for a pie.

time, beating well with a wooden spoon after each addition. (This beating is important as the gougère will not puff otherwise.) Stir in the diced cheese.

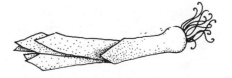

Pâte à Choux

1 cup sifted all-purpose flour
Pinch salt
Pinch pepper
1 cup water
8 tablespoons (1 stick) butter, cut up
4 eggs
⅛ pound sharp cheddar cheese, diced (approximately ½ cup)

1. Sift flour, salt, and pepper onto a sheet of wax paper. Heat water and butter in a large saucepan until the butter melts.
2. Turn up heat and bring water to boiling. Add flour mixture all at once and stir vigorously until mixture forms a ball in center of the pan. (This will take about a minute.)
3. Allow mixture to cool for 5 minutes. Add eggs one at a

Marcella Hazan's Ziti with Sausage and Cream Sauce

I suppose it's only natural and reasonable that you'll find better and more varied Italian food in Italy than you will in the U.S., with one important exception—Marcella Hazan. The food she serves in New York is as good or better than any I've sampled in Florence, Rome, or Venice. That's partly because, like the great reporter (as well as cook) she is, Marcella spends each summer in Italy, exploring the cuisines that vary so richly from region to region. I don't know where she found this ziti recipe—but it's the greatest!

Makes 8 servings

- 1 pound sweet Italian sausage
- 3 tablespoons chopped onion
- 2 tablespoons vegetable oil
- 3 tablespoons butter
- 1½ cups heavy cream
- ½ teaspoon salt
- ¼ teaspoon pepper
- 2 1-pound packages ziti
- ½ cup freshly grated parmesan cheese

1. Remove skin from the sausage.
2. Sauté onion in a large saucepan with oil and butter. When the onion turns pale gold, add sausage, crumbling it with a fork. Sauté, stirring occasionally, for 10 minutes.
3. Stir in cream, salt, and pepper. Continue cooking until cream mixture thickens, about 5 minutes.
4. Cook ziti, following package directions. Drain thoroughly. Transfer to a warm serving bowl, toss with all the sauce, and serve with a topping of grated parmesan cheese.

Marcella Hazan's Tripe and Beans

Tripe is a great favorite of mine, and here's a recipe that combines this delicate meat with beans and lots of good seasonings. It's Marcella Hazan's version of a popular Italian dish and, as she says, it's particularly easy to prepare because the tripe can be bought frozen, ready-to-cook— something new in convenience foods and a real joy to tripe lovers who once had to go through all kinds of tedious preliminary work to prepare the tripe for cooking. Since Marcella is a great Italian cook, you can be sure the dish is tasty. But it's also high in protein, and the tripe is low in calories and fat. What more could you ask?

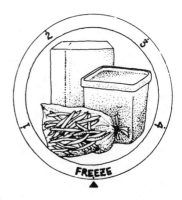

FREEZE

Makes 6 servings

1 whole carrot
1 celery stalk
1 whole onion, peeled
2 pounds frozen honeycomb tripe, thawed
4 tablespoons butter
⅓ cup olive oil
⅓ cup finely chopped onion
⅓ cup finely chopped celery
⅓ cup finely chopped carrot
½ teaspoon chopped rosemary
3 medium garlic cloves, peeled and cut into 2 or 3 pieces
2 tablespoons chopped parsley
1 cup dry white wine
3½ teaspoons salt
Pepper
1½ cups canned Italian plum tomatoes, coarsely chopped with their juice
1 cup homemade meat broth or ½ cup canned beef broth plus ½ cup water
1½ pounds fresh cranberry beans (unshelled weight) or 1 cup canned cannellini (white kidney beans)
1 cup freshly grated parmesan cheese

1. Choose a large, heavy casserole with a tight-fitting cover; put in carrot, celery stalk, and onion. Add 4 quarts of water and bring to a boil.
2. Wash tripe thoroughly in running water. Put it into the casserole; cover. When the water returns to a boil, cook for 20 minutes.
3. Lift out tripe and transfer it to a cutting board. Discard the rest of the contents of the casserole. As soon as the tripe is cool enough to handle, cut it into strips ½ inch wide. The length does not matter. Preheat oven to 350 degrees.
4. Rinse the casserole. Put in butter, olive oil, and chopped onion. Sauté onion lightly over medium heat. When onion has become faintly gold in color, add chopped celery and carrot; sauté lightly for about 1 minute.
5. Add the garlic, rosemary, parsley, and cut-up tripe. Cook for 2 or 3 minutes, stirring from time to time. Add wine; turn up heat and cook for about 30 seconds, or until the liquid has boiled away.
6. Add salt and a good sprinkling of pepper; stir thoroughly. Add tomatoes with juice and bring to a boil. Cover the pot and place it in the middle of preheated oven. Cook for at least 2 hours, checking the contents every 20 minutes to make sure there is still sufficient cooking liquid in the pot. If the liquid has evaporated, add about ⅓ cup of water. After 2 hours, the tripe

should be cooked. It is done when it is tender enough to be easily cut with a fork. Test it and taste it. Continue cooking, if necessary, until it is sufficiently tender.

7. If using fresh beans, they must be cooked before the tripe is done. If using canned beans, they can be added at step 9 when the tripe has finished cooking. For fresh beans, shell the beans, and rinse in cold water. Put them in a pot with enough water to cover by about 1½ inches. Do *not* add any salt.

8. Bring beans to a very slow boil; cover the pot. If the beans are very fresh and young they will cook in about 45 minutes. Otherwise they may take as much as 1 to 1½ hours. When tender, turn off heat and let them rest in their own cooking liquid.

9. When the tripe is done, remove from the oven. If using fresh beans, add the beans plus ¼ cup of their cooking liquid, or add the canned beans. Transfer the casserole to a burner; cover, and simmer for 5 to 10 minutes.

10. Off the heat, mix in parmesan cheese. Serve from the casserole, piping hot.

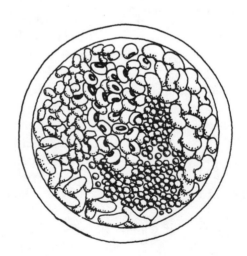

Marcella Hazan's All-Seafood Fish Soup

When Marcella Hazan sent me this recipe, she said, "it's a lovely dish for people who like fish soup, but who don't like fishbones." I qualify, and while the soup has a nice variety of seafood in it, you'll find nary a bone (the combination consists of shrimp, mussels, clams, and squid). When making it, just be sure to use fresh clams and mussels, and, if available, fresh shrimp and squid. (If not, use frozen.)

Makes 6 servings

2 pounds squid
2 dozen small littleneck clams
2 pounds mussels
⅔ cup olive oil
½ cup chopped onion
1 tablespoon chopped garlic
3 tablespoons chopped parsley
1 cup dry white wine
1½ cups canned Italian plum tomatoes, cut up, with their juice
1 pound shrimp
  Salt
  Pepper

1. To prepare the squid for cooking, first separate the tentacles from the sac. Hold the sac in one hand, and firmly pull off the tentacles with the other. Cut the tentacles straight across above the eyes, and discard everything from the eyes down. Divide the tentacles into two clusters. Remove the thin bone from the sac, and thoroughly rinse out the inside of the sac clearing it of anything it may contain. Peel off the sac's outer skin. (It is easiest to do this under cold running water.) Wash all the sacs and tentacles in several changes of cold water. Drain and pat dry thoroughly. Cut the sacs into rings ½-inch wide, and set everything aside.

2. Soak the clams in a basin full of cold water for several minutes. Empty out the water; refill the basin and scrub the clams, either with a coarse brush, or by rubbing one clam forcefully against another. When finished, drain and refill the basin; scrub clams again. Repeat the entire operation several times until water runs perfectly clear. Set the clams aside in a bowl.

3. Clean the mussels using the same procedure as for the clams. In addition, trim off with a sharp knife the wisps of rope that may protrude from the shells. Set the mussels aside in a bowl.

4. Put all the clams in a covered pot over high heat. (Use a steamer pot or large pot with just enough water to cover clams.) As the clams open up, remove them; leave just 6 clams attached to their shells. Separate the rest from the shells. Put the shelled clam meat in a small bowl.

5. Carefully filter all the clam juice in the pot through cheesecloth, then pour it into the bowl containing the shelled clam meat.

6. Repeat the same operation with the mussels. After the mussels have opened, set aside 6 nice, large mussels without shelling them, and shell the rest. Put the shelled mussel meat in a small bowl; cover with the mussels' pan juices filtered in the same manner as the clam juice.

7. Put oil and chopped onion into a deep saucepan. Sauté onion over medium-high heat until it is translucent.

8. Add garlic. When garlic becomes lightly colored, add parsley. Stir rapidly once or twice, then add wine. Allow wine to boil for about 30 seconds, then add tomatoes with juice. Cook at a steady simmer for 10 minutes.

9. Add squid. Add clam juice, leaving just enough in the bowl to cover the clams. Do the same with the mussel juice. Cover the pan, setting the cover slightly askew, and cook at a gentle simmer for 45 minutes, or until the squid is very tender when pricked by a fork.

10. While the squid is cooking, shell, de-vein, and wash shrimp.

11. When squid is done, season liberally with salt and pepper. Add shrimp and cook for 3 to 4 minutes on high heat, stirring from time to time. Add all clam meat with its juice, mussel meat with its juice,

and unshelled clams and mussels. Cook for 1 more minute. Serve immediately with plenty of good, crusty bread on the side.

Veal Scallopine with Marsala and Cream

This recipe is a departure from most veal scallopine dishes because it uses cream in addition to the usual ingredients. The reason Marcella Hazan added this to the recipe, she says, is that "the cream softens some of the marsala's brashness while robbing it of none of its flavor, and turns this into a rather more gentle dish than it is in its standard edition." This imaginativeness is what I love about so many of Marcella's recipes. And, true to form, she suggests you serve the scallopine with almost any vegetable except those in a tomato sauce. Particularly fitting would be to sauté the vegetable with butter and cheese. The thought of it all makes me very hungry.

Makes 4 servings

- 2 tablespoons vegetable oil
- 3 tablespoons butter
- 1¼ pounds thin veal scallopine (see Note)
- 5 tablespoons flour, spread on a dish
  Salt
  Pepper to taste
- ½ cup dry marsala
- ⅓ cup heavy cream

1. Put oil and butter in a large sauté pan or skillet and heat over high heat.
2. Dredge a few pieces of scallopine, one at a time and on both sides, in flour. As the butter foam begins to subside, put scallopine in pan. Do not put in any more than will fit without overlapping.
3. Brown the scallopine quickly on both sides. Thirty seconds or so for each side is quite sufficient if the cooking fat is hot enough. Try to turn and brown the meat in the pan so that all the scallopine will be cooked evenly. When the scallopine are done, transfer to a platter large enough to hold them without overlapping. Use more than one platter if necessary.
4. As scallopine are removed from the pan, replace them with the raw scallopine that remain, dredging them in flour just

before putting them in the pan. When all the meat is done and has been transferred to the platter, turn off heat under the pan. Season meat with salt and pepper to taste.

5. Add marsala to the pan, turning the heat on again to high. Scrape the cooking residues loose from the bottom of the pan; stir. When you see that the marsala has begun to boil away, add cream. Stir constantly over high heat until cream is bound with juices in the pan into a thick, dark sauce.

6. Turn heat down to medium; put into the pan all the scallopine, one at a time, turning each one over in the sauce. Turn off the heat as soon as the last of the scallopine has been put into the pan.

7. Transfer the scallopine to a heated serving platter. Pour over them all the sauce from the pan.

Note: The very best scallopine come from a single muscle in the hind leg called the top round. Whether you cut them yourself at home or the butcher does it, they should be cut by slicing the meat against the grain. If they are cut along the grain, they will shrivel and curl while cooking. They can be as thick as ⅜ inch when cut. Then they should be flattened with a meat pounding tool or the flat side of a heavy cleaver.

Marcella Hazan's Fricasseed Chicken with Lemon

"Nearly all Italian chicken dishes have these things in common: they are quick, uncomplicated, and make a judiciously sparing use of seasonings," notes Marcella Hazan. "And their appeal is equally great for those who eat them and those who prepare them because they tax neither the palates of the former or the patience of the latter," she adds. This recipe fits the description and owes these merits to Marcella.

Makes 4 servings

- 1 whole chicken (2½–3 pounds)
- 2 tablespoons vegetable oil
- 1 tablespoon butter
- 1 sprig of rosemary or 1 teaspoon dried rosemary leaves
- 3 whole garlic cloves, peeled
  Salt
  Pepper
- ⅓ cup dry white wine
- 2 tablespoons freshly squeezed lemon juice
- 5–6 thin, julienne strips lemon peel

1. Cut up chicken into 6 pieces; wash under cold running water. Do *not* dry them. Put chicken pieces skin side down in a sauté pan in which they will fit without overlapping. Turn the heat to medium-high, drying and lightly browning the chicken on all sides. No cooking fat is required at this point. The moisture clinging to the washed chicken pieces and their own fat will suffice. You must watch them, however, and turn them before they stick to the pan.
2. When the chicken is lightly browned on all sides, add oil, butter, rosemary, garlic, salt, and pepper. Cook for 2 to 3 minutes, turning once or twice.
3. Add wine; turn the heat up a bit and let the wine bubble for about 30 seconds. Turn the heat down to medium-low; cover pan. Cook until chicken is

tender, testing one of the thighs with a fork. It should take about 35 to 40 minutes.
4. Turn off heat and transfer just the chicken pieces to a warm serving platter.
5. Tip the pan and with a spoon remove all but 2 tablespoons fat. Add lemon juice and lemon peel; turn heat on to medium-low. Stir with a wooden spoon, scraping loose any cooking juices that have stuck to the pan. Pour this light sauce over the chicken and serve at once.

Marcella's Spaghetti with Fish-Head Sauce

"For some unaccountable reason, most people assume that a fish's head, while it may originally have been important to the fish, is of negligible interest as food. Quite the contrary is true. There is no part of the fish that is as sweet-tasting and flavorful as those delectable morsels concealed in the head." Well, fish heads are not a particular turn-on for me, but this recipe goes to show how right Marcella Hazan is. Made exclusively with fish heads, it's a really tasty, appealing pasta sauce.

Makes 8 servings

⅔ cup olive oil
⅓ cup chopped onion
1 tablespoon chopped garlic
4 tablespoons chopped parsley
3 assorted fish heads, from such fish as sea bass, red snapper, porgie, etc., washed in cold water
⅓ cup dry white wine
1½ cups canned Italian plum tomatoes, cut up, with their juice
Salt
Pepper
2 1-pound packages spaghetti
3 tablespoons butter

1. Choose a saucepan that can later contain all the heads without overlapping. Put in oil and onion; sauté onion over medium heat until it is translucent.
2. Add garlic and sauté until it becomes lightly colored.

3. Add half the chopped parsley. Stir once or twice; add the fish heads.
4. Turn the heads once, coating them well; add wine and turn up heat to high. When wine has bubbled away for about 30 seconds, add cut-up tomatoes with juice and turn the heat down to medium.
5. Add salt and pepper; cook for 15 to 20 minutes, depending on the size of the heads, turning from time to time.
6. Remove heads from the pan. With a small spoon scoop out all the bits of meat in the heads, such as under the cheeks, next to the neck, and so on. Put the meat aside on a small dish.
7. Remove all the larger bones and discard. Take a food mill fitted with a disk with very small holes, and pass the remains of

the heads through it into the saucepan.

8. Turn heat to medium-low and cook at a very gentle simmer for about 30 minutes, stirring from time to time, until sauce thickens to a dense, creamy consistency. Add bits of meat that were set aside. Cook for 5 minutes longer, stirring the sauce a few times. Turn off heat.

9. Cook the spaghetti in abundant salted water until done al dente, very firm to the bite. Drain; transfer to a heated serving bowl and toss with the sauce, mixing in the remaining chopped parsley and butter. Serve at once.

Fillet of Beef Wellington

I can't think of any food more representative of Texas than beef. But, unfortunately, most of us only think of barbecued beef when mention of the Lone Star state is made, forgetting that Texas hospitality and inventiveness go far beyond this expected backyard favorite. Fillet of Beef Wellington, for instance, is a sophisticated, beautiful entrée; here's how it's made at the famous Sakowitz Department Store restaurant in Houston.

Makes 6 servings

3 pounds fillet of beef (12 inches long)
1 teaspoon salt
⅛ teaspoon pepper
4 tablespoon (½ stick) butter, softened
½ cup chopped celery
1 medium onion, chopped (½ cup)
¼ cup chopped parsley
1 bay leaf
Pinch of leaf rosemary, crumbled
½ cup dry white wine
1 cup Chicken Liver Pâté (recipe follows)
1 package piecrust mix
1 egg, lightly beaten
Béarnaise Sauce (recipe follows)

1. Trim fat from fillet; tie with string at about 1½-inch intervals to retain shape. Rub with salt and pepper; spread with butter. Spread a 15½ by 10½-by-1-inch jelly-roll pan with vegetables, bay leaf, and rosemary; place fillet on top.

2. Roast in a very hot oven, 450 degrees, for 15 to 25 minutes for rare, depending on thickness of fillet. (For medium-rare, roast for 10 minutes longer. Beef Wellington is best served rare or medium.)

3. Remove fillet from oven; cool. Wrap in foil and refrigerate 4 hours or overnight.
4. Pour wine into pan and place over low heat. Simmer gently a few minutes; strain and reserve for preparing béarnaise sauce.
5. Cut strings from chilled fillet; spread with chicken liver pâté.
6. Prepare piecrust mix, following directions on label for two-crust pie. Roll out on lightly floured surface so pastry is 4 inches longer than fillet and about 3 times wider (pastry must overlap for seal).
7. Place fillet on pastry, top side down; bring long sides up to overlap along the bottom of fillet. Seal edges with egg. Trim end of pastry; fold in and seal with egg. Place fillet on jellyroll pan, seam side down.
8. Brush pastry with beaten egg. Reroll pastry scraps; cut into small decorative shapes. Arrange small cutouts down center of fillet; brush cutouts with egg.
9. Bake in a hot oven, 425 degrees, for 30 minutes, or until pastry is golden brown. Remove to serving platter; serve with béarnaise sauce.

Chicken Liver Pâté

Makes about 1 cup

8 tablespoons (1 stick) butter
½ pound chicken livers
1 small onion, chopped (¼ cup)
⅛ teaspoon salt
  Pinch of pepper
2 teaspoons brandy

1. Melt 2 tablespoons of butter in a skillet. Add livers, onion, salt, and pepper. Cover; cook for 5 minutes, or until livers are firm but still pink inside.

2. Cool mixture slightly; put into electric blender. Whirl until smooth, stopping blender to scrape sides of container often. Add remaining butter and brandy. Chill.

Béarnaise Sauce

Makes about ¾ cup

¼ cup tarragon vinegar
Reserved pan liquid from Beef Wellington
3 shallots, peeled and chopped
3 peppercorns, crushed
⅛ teaspoon leaf thyme, crumbled
2 eggs yolks
8 tablespoons (1 stick) butter, melted
⅛ teaspoon leaf tarragon, crumbled
⅛ teaspoon leaf chervil, crumbled

1. Put vinegar into top of double boiler. Remove fat from top of pan liquid. Measure ¼ cup of liquid; add to vinegar. Add shallots, crushed pepper, and thyme.
2. Simmer mixture over direct heat until reduced to ⅓ original volume. Strain; there should be just under ¼ cup of liquid. Cool.

3. Return liquid to top of double boiler. Beat egg yolks just to mix; add to liquid. Place over hot, not boiling, water. Use wire whisk to beat in melted butter, a little at a time. Continue whisking until sauce is thickened and velvety in texture. Add tarragon and chervil. Serve at once.

Note: If sauce becomes too thick and separates, whisk in a little hot water until it becomes smooth again.

Josette King's Spinach and Egg Casserole

Josette King from Wakefield, Massachusetts, makes a delicious casserole she calls oeufs à la florentine. *Since my French isn't very good, I simply call it spinach and egg casserole. But no matter how you say it, it's an inexpensive and satisfying meal all by itself.*

Makes 6 servings

 7 tablespoons butter
1½ teaspoons salt
 ⅜ teaspoon pepper
 ⅛ teaspoon ground nutmeg
 2 packages (10 ounces each) frozen chopped spinach, thawed long enough to be cut into ½-inch chunks
 1 medium onion, chopped (½ cup)
 3 tablespoons flour
 2 cups hot milk
 ½ cup shredded swiss cheese (2 ounces)
12 hard-boiled eggs

1. Melt 3 tablespoons butter in a small skillet. Add ½ teaspoon salt, ⅛ teaspoon pepper, ⅛ teaspoon nutmeg, and spinach. Cover; cook slowly for 3 minutes, or until spinach has thawed completely. Remove cover; raise heat to high and evaporate all extra moisture.

2. Melt 4 tablespoons butter in a saucepan and sauté onion until tender. Sprinkle in flour and cook, stirring constantly, until mixture bubbles. Stir in milk; bring to boiling, stirring constantly. Remove from heat and stir in cheese and remaining salt and pepper.

3. Mix half the cheese sauce into the spinach until well blended. Place spinach in a buttered 8-cup casserole; top with quartered hard-boiled eggs. Cover with remaining sauce.

4. Bake in a very slow oven, 250 degrees, for about 10 minutes. (Do not allow to brown or it will overcook the eggs and make them rubbery.)

Best of the Best Vegetables

John Clancy's Fabulous Fried Onion Rings
Jean Anderson's French Fried Potatoes
My Own Home-Fried Potatoes
Marian Burros' Corn Roasted in Foil
Ann Seranne's Three-Day Sauerkraut
Ann Seranne's Cabbage Rolls
Nika Hazelton's Ratatouille
James Beard's Spinach Roll with Creamed
    Mushrooms
Mimi Sheraton's Pork and Beans

John Clancy's Fabulous Fried Onion Rings

This is a deceiving recipe. It's called fried onion rings, which is what cooking teacher John Clancy started with when he devised the basic beer batter recipe. But if you look at the variations listed at the end of the directions, you'll see he's taken this idea one step further—the batter can be used for frying zucchini, eggplant, and apples as well as onions. The batter works well for many things because it's light and delicate and because John's technique for frying prevents greasy results. The onion rings are still my favorite beer batter vegetable, served with steak, or alone as a snack; but I think you'll enjoy trying his variations too.

Makes 6 servings

1½ cups all-purpose flour
1½ cups beer, active or flat, cold or at room temperature
 3 very large yellow or Bermuda onions
3–4 cups shortening

1. Sift flour into a large bowl. Gradually mix beer into flour with a wooden spoon. Cover bowl and allow batter to sit at room temperature for 3 hours. (During the 3-hour "rest" period the gluten, a sticky, high protein substance in the flour, is broken down by the alcohol in the beer. This creates a very light, delicate batter.)

2. About 20 minutes before the batter is ready, preheat the oven to 200 degrees. Place heavy brown paper or layers of paper toweling on a jelly-roll pan. Carefully peel the onions so as not to cut into the outer layer. Slice them ¼ inch thick. Separate the slices into rings and set aside. On top of the stove, melt enough shortening in a 10-inch skillet to come 2 inches up the sides of the pan. Heat shortening to 375 degrees (use a deep-frying thermometer).

3. With metal tongs, dip onion rings, a few at a time, into batter. Carefully place them in the hot fat. Fry, turning once

or twice, until onions are an even, delicate golden color. Transfer rings to paper-lined jelly-roll pan.

4. To keep warm, place them on the middle shelf of the preheated oven until all the onion rings have been fried. The rings stay crisp for several hours at room temperature and taste great even after they've cooled off. However, they may be reheated successfully. Place them in a 400-degree oven for 4 to 6 minutes.

Variations

CRISPY ZUCCHINI STICKS
Cut the ends off 5 very small, unpeeled zucchini. Cut into quarters, lengthwise, then into slivers. *Do not salt.* Dip, fry, and keep warm, as for onion rings. Serve hot.

FRIED EGGPLANT FINGERS
Cut ends off 2 small, unpeeled eggplants. Cut lengthwise into ½-inch slices; cut slices in half, crosswise. Cut pieces into ½-inch fingers. *Do not salt.* Dip, fry, and keep warm, as for onion rings. Serve hot.

GOLDEN APPLE RINGS
Use Rome Beauty or Golden Delicious varieties. Pare and core 3 apples; cut into ½-inch rings.

Generously sprinkle cinnamon-sugar on wax paper. Place apples on paper and sprinkle top of apples with more cinnamon-sugar. Dip, fry, and keep warm, as for onion rings. Serve warm. Sprinkle with confectioners sugar at serving time (not ahead of time, or they will go limp).

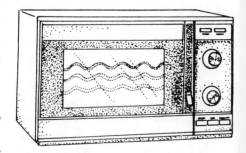

Jean Anderson's French Fried Potatoes

When I asked Jean Anderson for her recipe for french fried potatoes, I wasn't surprised when I received not only the recipe, but also some notes on how her technique differs from others' as well as some helpful tips to keep in mind. Jean is always this thorough, and it's part of the reason she's such a terrific food reporter— as well as a distinguished travel wri-

ter and author of many highly respected cookbooks. The latest of these, The Doubleday Cookbook, *took eight years to complete, and it was well worth waiting for.*

Her french fries are worth waiting for too. Jean suggests starting by using Russet Burbanks (better known as "Idahos") because these potatoes have an exceptionally fine flavor, an elongated shape that lends itself to being cut in long, thin strips, and a texture that makes them cook quickly and get crisp without absorbing undue cooking fat. Also, her technique calls for double-frying, which means that you can parfry the potatoes several hours ahead of time if you want, then finish frying just before serving. It's a convenient method and one that guarantees crisp, golden, grease-free, tender fries. And that's the way I like them.

Makes 4 to 6 servings

---

10 large Idaho potatoes of uniform size (they should be firm, free of blemishes, sprouts and green "sunburn" patches)
Vegetable oil or shortening for deep fat frying (approximately 2 quarts oil or 2 pounds shortening)
Salt

1. Have ready a large bowl of ice water (this not only keeps the freshly cut potatoes from darkening, but also makes them crisp). Scrub potatoes well in tepid water and pat dry. Peel potatoes, one at a time; slice lengthwise about ⅜ inch thick. Cut each slice into strips about ⅜ inch wide. Immerse immediately in ice water. When all potatoes have been cut, soak for 5 minutes in ice water—no longer or potatoes may absorb too much moisture and turn limp in the frying.

2. Place mesh frying basket in deep-fat fryer. Insert deep-fat thermometer, add vegetable oil or shortening, and begin heating.

3. Meanwhile, pat potato strips as dry as possible. When fat has reached 375 degrees, place about ¼ of the potatoes into the fryer basket. Immerse in the hot fat and fry just until the color of pale ivory, about 4 to 5 minutes.

4. Spread potatoes out on several thicknesses of paper toweling at once and toss lightly so that all excess fat is absorbed. Continue parfrying potatoes, raising or lowering burner heat as needed to keep the temperature of fat as nearly at 375 degrees as possible. (If temperature drops too low, the potatoes are apt to absorb too much fat and become greasy. If it becomes too hot, they will brown before they have cooked through to the center.) When all potatoes have been parfried, spread out

on fresh layers of paper toweling and let stand, uncovered, at room temperature until ready to finish frying.

5. For the second frying, heat the fat to 390 degrees. Take about ¼ of the potatoes at a time and fry just until golden brown and crisp, about 1 to 2 minutes. Keep them crisp and hot while frying the remaining potatoes by spreading them out on a large, paper-towel-lined metal tray and setting them, uncovered, in a slow oven, 300 degrees.

6. Sprinkle the french fries with salt and serve. The American way is, of course, to douse the french fries with ketchup. The French like to dip theirs in mustard, and the British prefer drizzlings of vinegar.

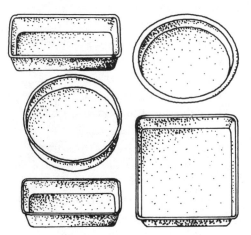

My Own Home-Fried Potatoes

I've always loved home fries and have my own special way of making them. This recipe is very basic and easy, but the technique varies from other home-fry recipes, and it makes a big difference in the end result. For instance, unlike some recipes, I start with raw baking potatoes. (The long, lean ones are just right because they give the best-size slices.) Then, I slice the potatoes very thinly so they'll fry crisply and put them in a combination of butter and vegetable oil for the cooking fat. This is a trick chefs use to give foods the smoke-resistant qualities of oil-fried foods while maintaining the flavor of butter-fried foods. Also, to get the potatoes crisp, I don't turn them often.

Makes 4 servings

2 large or 4 medium Idaho potatoes (approximately 1½ pounds)
3 tablespoons butter
3 tablespoons vegetable oil
1 medium onion, thinly sliced and separated into rings
  Salt
  Pepper

1. Pare potatoes; cut into very thin slices. Heat butter and vegetable oil in a heavy 10-inch skillet until a few drops of water will sizzle when flicked into skillet.
2. Spread a thin layer of sliced potatoes in the hot fat; allow to cook until the slices of potato turn a golden brown, about 5 minutes. Layer onion rings and remaining potato slices in skillet. Turn potatoes with a broad, flat turner. Allow potatoes to cook until crispy-golden; then turn again.
3. Continue cooking and turning until potatoes are crisp and brown. Sprinkle with salt and pepper. Serve at once.

Marian Burros' Corn Roasted in Foil

When I told food writer and editor Marian Burros how much I like barbecuing, she gave me this recipe, along with some advice. Make plenty, she said, because everyone will be back for more. You know, she's right.

Makes 4 servings (2 ears each)

1 quart water
2 tablespoons sugar
8 ears corn, in husks
8 tablespoons (1 stick) butter, melted
Seasoned salt or table salt

1. Combine water and sugar in a large roasting pan. Add corn and soak for 15 minutes. Remove from water and wrap each ear, still in its husk, in a piece of aluminum foil. Twist ends to close.
2. Place wrapped corn on grill, 5 inches from heat, and roast for 15 to 20 minutes, turning often.
3. Remove foil, strip husks from corn (use some kind of protective gloves), and roll in shallow platter of melted butter seasoned with salt.

Ann Seranne's Three-Day Sauerkraut

When food writer Ann Seranne gave me this recipe she said the credit should really go to her father. "My father was no cook," Ann added, "but there were three things he liked to make. He liked to pan-fry a freshly caught trout, sauté a few field mushrooms in butter to serve on a slice of buttered toast, and make sauerkraut."

Ann says that one of her earliest memories is of tons of cabbage tumbling down the coal chute into the family's furnace cellar to be made into kraut. "It was a real production line," she noted. "Dad would shred the cabbage, mother would salt it, and the three of us children would take turns tamping down the cabbage in the kegs, until the juices began to run. After about ten days of fermenting, the kegs were rolled into the cold cellar and seldom a day went by that a casserole of sauerkraut did not accompany dinner.

"Of course, few people today are going to make sauerkraut in any quantity, but a small batch is easy to make in any home kitchen." And here's the recipe for doing so.

Makes about 8 quarts

8 pounds cabbage
8 tablespoons pickling salt (1 tablespoon per pound of cabbage)
  Boiling water

1. Core and shred the cabbage, discarding any discolored outer leaves. Layer about 2 pounds of the shredded cabbage in a crock and sprinkle with 2 tablespoons salt. Repeat the layers until all the cabbage and salt are used.
2. Place a heavy dinner plate upside down on top of the cabbage and weigh the plate down with a brick or other heavy weight. Add boiling water to cover cabbage and plate. Cover crock and leave in a warm kitchen for 3 or 4 days. In 48 hours the cabbage will have fermented into young kraut; in 72 hours it will be the real thing. Cover well and store in the refrigerator (up to 1 month).

Ann Seranne's Cabbage Rolls

One of the best ways to use Three-Day Sauerkraut (see previous recipe) is in the following recipe.

Makes 8 to 10 servings

1 head cabbage
1½ pounds ground lean veal or beef
¾ pound ground lean pork
1 medium onion, chopped
2 large cloves garlic, chopped
6 tablespoons vegetable oil
2 teaspoons salt
1½ teaspoons coarsely ground pepper
½ cup raw rice
1 teaspoon dry dillweed
1 egg
1 cup cream
1 large onion, chopped
1 bay leaf
1 6-ounce can tomato paste
2 teaspoons paprika
4 cups water
4 pounds sauerkraut
 Sour cream

1. Place cabbage in a large saucepan, with enough water to cover cabbage. Cover and simmer for about 10 minutes, or until leaves are transparent. Remove cabbage from water to drain and cool.

2. Combine ground meats, the medium chopped onion, garlic, 2 tablespoons of the oil, salt, 1 teaspoon of the pepper, rice, dillweed, egg, and cream in a large mixing bowl.

3. Remove core from cabbage and separate the leaves. Cut away the thick stems and cut the leaves into pieces about 6 inches long and 4 inches wide. Put about 2 tablespoons of the meat mixture on one end of each piece of cabbage, roll up and tuck in the ends. (Meat stuffs about 40 leaves.)

4. Sauté the large chopped onion in 4 tablespoons of oil in a large skillet until soft, but not brown. Add bay leaf, tomato paste, paprika, remaining pepper, and the water. Bring to a boil, stirring until tomato paste is mixed with the liquid.

5. Put half the sauerkraut (2 pounds) in a colander to drain. Rinse lightly under cool water and empty into a large heavy casserole or Dutch oven. Pour the tomato paste liquid over the sauerkraut and arrange the cabbage rolls on top. Drain and rinse the remaining 2 pounds of sauerkraut and spread on top of the cabbage rolls. Cover casserole and bring to a boil. Lower heat, simmer for 30 minutes, then transfer to a slow oven, 300 degrees, and cook for 2½ to 3 hours. Check occasionally and add boiling water if needed to keep ingredients well moistened with liquid. Serve with sour cream.

Nika Hazelton's Ratatouille

Ratatouille is a really versatile French vegetable stew that can be served either hot or cold. And I like it best when it's made several days ahead of time because the flavors really have a chance to blend thoroughly. When preparing the recipe, you'll notice that no liquid is added to the mixture as it cooks. This may seem unusual, but Nika Hazelton explained to me it's because the vegetables have so much natural water in them that comes out during cooking. As a matter of fact, you may have to remove the cover for a while to let the juices cook down. Otherwise, the ratatouille may be too liquid, and who wants to spoil a good thing!

Makes 6 servings

- 2 large onions, peeled and thinly sliced
- 2 cloves garlic, mashed
- 1 medium eggplant, peeled and cut into ½-inch cubes
- 6 medium zucchini or yellow squashes, thickly sliced
- 2 large green or red sweet peppers, halved, seeded, and cut into strips
- 4 large fresh tomatoes, peeled and chopped
- 1½–2 teaspoons salt
  Pepper to taste
- 2 tablespoons fresh chopped basil or 2 teaspoons dried basil
- ½ cup minced parsley
- 6 tablespoons olive oil

1. Layer onions, garlic, eggplant, zucchini, peppers, and tomatoes into a 5- or 6-quart casserole, sprinkling each layer with a little salt, pepper, basil, and parsley. Press vegetables down tightly, pour the olive oil over all, and cover tightly.
2. Cook on top of the stove, over very low heat for 2 to 3 hours, or until vegetables are very soft, but still have some shape. Or bake in moderate oven, 350 degrees, for about the same time.
3. During cooking or baking, baste top vegetables several times with pan juices. If ratatouille is quite soupy, cook uncovered for the last hour. When done, mix gently with a fork; taste and add more seasoning, if needed.

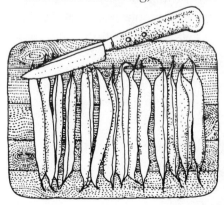

James Beard's Spinach Roll with Creamed Mushrooms

This is an economical dish and, like so many of James Beard's recipes, it's very easy to prepare. There should be no doubt either that it's good because when it comes to fine food, James Beard is in a class all his own. Along with only two or three others, he's the premier writer in the entire food business, and as a cooking teacher, his reputation is hard to equal. With recipes such as this, I can see why.

Makes 6 servings

3 packages (10 ounces each) frozen spinach
¼ cup packaged bread crumbs
2 teaspoons salt
¾ teaspoon pepper
  Pinch of ground nutmeg
6 tablespoons butter, melted
4 eggs, separated
6 tablespoons grated parmesan cheese
¾ pound mushrooms, sliced
4 tablespoons butter
3 tablespoons flour
¾ cup heavy cream
2 tablespoons chopped parsley

1. Thaw spinach in a large skillet over low heat; drain and chop.

Butter a 15-by-10-by-1-inch jelly-roll pan; line with wax paper. Butter again and sprinkle with bread crumbs.

2. When spinach is cool enough to handle, squeeze out all excess water. Place spinach in a bowl; add 1 teaspoon salt, ¼ teaspoon pepper, nutmeg and melted butter.

3. Beat in egg yolks one at a time. Beat egg whites in a small bowl until they hold soft peaks; fold into spinach mixture. Spoon mixture into prepared pan and smooth the top evenly with a spatula. Sprinkle with 4 tablespoons parmesan cheese.

4. Bake in a moderate oven, 350 degrees, for 12 minutes, or until the center feels barely firm when touched lightly.

5. While roll is baking, sauté mushrooms quickly in 4 tablespoons butter in a large skillet. Shake the skillet occasionally. Sprinkle mushrooms with flour, 1 teaspoon salt, and ½ teaspoon pepper; stir in cream. Mix gently in the pan just until thickened.

6. When roll is baked, place a sheet of buttered wax paper, butter side down, over the roll; invert onto a warm cooky sheet. Carefully remove bottom paper.

7. Spread mushroom mixture over hot spinach roll. Roll up, jelly-roll fashion, starting at a short

end and using the paper to aid in rolling. Ease the roll onto a warm platter, seam side down.

8. Sprinkle roll with remaining cheese and parsley.

Mimi Sheraton's Pork and Beans

There are some basic foods I would never dream of preparing from scratch, either because they're too complicated or too readily available in a package. But with baked beans I make an exception. And one of the best recipes for homemade pork and beans is from Mimi Sheraton's kitchen.

Makes 10 to 12 servings

2½ pounds pea or navy beans
1 pound lean salt pork
1½ cups molasses
¼ cup white vinegar
1 tablespoon salt
1 tablespoon dry mustard
1½ teaspoons black pepper
1 large onion, studded with 4–5 whole cloves

1. Soak beans, following package directions; drain. Place beans in a large kettle; cover with water. Bring to boiling, lower heat, and cover kettle. Simmer for 1½ hours, or until beans are almost tender, but before skins burst; drain.

2. While beans simmer, cover salt pork with water in a large saucepan. Bring to boiling; simmer for 10 minutes. Drain on paper towels. Cut 3 thin slices from slab and cut slices into large dices. Score rind on the remaining slab.

3. Combine molasses, vinegar, salt, mustard, and pepper in a small bowl.

4. Place ⅓ of the diced pork in the bottom of an 18-cup earthenware bean pot. Add about ⅓ of the beans and molasses mixture. Add more pork bits and continue layering beans, molasses mixture, and pork until pot is almost full. Bury onion in the middle of the pot. Add scored pork, burying most of it in the top layer of beans. Add enough boiling water to come to the level of beans; cover.

5. Bake in a very slow oven, 275 degrees, for 5 to 7 hours, adding more boiling water during baking if top beans become dry. Bake uncovered for the last 30 to 45 minutes, so rind will become crisp.

Best of the Best Sandwiches, Side Dishes, and Snacks

Betty Jacobson's Cucumber and Onion Sandwiches
Lucy Snow's Tuna Fish Sandwiches
Mimi Sheraton's Sabrett-Style Hot Dogs
 and Onions
Italian Street Festa Sausages
Fried Sausages with Peppers and Onions
Real Texas Tacos
Brennan's Eggs Hussarde
Lea Rabin's Blintzes
Burt Reynolds' Parmesan Garlic Toast
Saratoga Potato Chips

Betty Jacobson's Cucumber and Onion Sandwiches

Betty Jacobson and her husband are close friends of mine and I've enjoyed some delightful times with them, particularly the days we've spent aboard their motorboat, The Gitana, *exploring Long Island Sound. Betty's menus on-board often included this simple but delicious cucumber-and-onion combination. I wangled the recipe from her with the promise that next time we get out on the water, I'll make the sandwiches—using her recipe, of course.*

Cucumber
Red onion
White bread (very thin slices)
Salt
Pepper
Mayonnaise

1. Peel cucumber and red onion and slice both very thinly.
2. Place a layer of cucumber and a layer of onion on 1 slice of bread. Add salt and pepper to taste.
3. Spread second slice of bread with desired amount of mayonnaise and close sandwich. Repeat to make as many sandwiches as you like.

Lucy Snow's Tuna Fish Sandwiches

If it seems like a put-on to publish a recipe for tuna fish, then you haven't had Ceil Dyer's version of this popular sandwich. Ceil is a collector of good recipes and spends a lot of time in her Pinehurst, North Carolina, home writing food features and books, including the popular After Hours Parties Cookbook. *Anyway, when she gave me this recipe, she told me about Lucy Snow for whom it's named.*

"Lucy Snow," says Ceil, "lived down the street from us in Shreveport, Louisiana. She was, as we politely put it in those days, an elderly single lady. She looked a little like Edna May Oliver, always wore a hat placed straight on her head and drove a black Model-T Ford. She was my mother's best friend, which goes to prove that opposites attract: Mother was young, never wore a hat, had been married twice, and everyone said she looked like Myrna Loy.

"Miss Snow's tuna fish sandwiches were considered the best, always in demand for weddings and 'silver teas,' and she taught mother how to make them. Mother, being mother, let me help by chopping the celery and pickles; she would sit on a kitch-

en stool and watch to make sure I had chopped them sufficiently fine. 'No,' she would say, 'that's not fine enough, they must be very fine if our sandwiches are to be good.' She was right, of course, and to this day I have never tasted a better sandwich than Miss Lucy's tuna fish."

Makes 14 sandwiches

28 very thin slices firm, white bread (1-pound loaf minus ends)
8 tablespoons (1 stick) butter
1 cup firmly packed, finely minced celery (6–8 stalks)
1 8-ounce jar sweet mixed pickles, drained
1 7-ounce can tuna fish
4 heaping tablespoons mayonnaise (3½–4 ounces)
2 teaspoons prepared mustard
1 tablespoon fresh lemon juice
⅛ teaspoon salt

1. Place wrapped loaf of bread in freezer to firm slices while preparing filling. Place butter in a small bowl and let stand at room temperature until very soft.

2. Mince celery till exceedingly fine, so fine it will mound on a spoon; place in mixing bowl. Mince pickles as finely as celery.

3. Dump tuna fish into bowl. Using fork shred finely into celery and pickles.

4. Add enough mayonnaise to hold mixture together, mustard, lemon juice, and salt. Stir with a fork to blend. Refrigerate filling while preparing bread.

5. Whip softened butter till light and fluffy. Remove bread from freezer and spread each slice with thin layer of butter.

6. Spread about 2 heaping tea-spoons of filling evenly on half of bread slices. Cover with remaining slices. Stack sandwiches (3 or 4 to a stack) and cut crusts from bread with a serrated knife. Cut sandwiches in half.

7. Rinse clean tea towel or large napkin in cold water, wring out till just damp dry. Place towel on large plate, stack sandwiches on it; fold napkin over sandwiches to form a neat package. Refrigerate two hours or longer before serving.

Note: Sandwiches will stay fresh for several days in refrigerator. If towel becomes completely dry, moisten very lightly with cold water. To take on a picnic, place cold, moist towel-wrapped sandwiches in plastic bag or wrap in foil and place on top of ice in ice bucket.

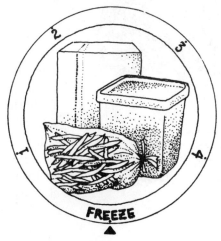

Mimi Sheraton's Sabrett-Style Hot Dogs and Onions

Food writer and gourmet Mimi Sheraton recently confessed that she's a hot-dog freak. "I have been almost constitutionally unable to resist them for as long as I can remember," she admits. She says that the ones served outdoors by street vendors are her favorites.

But Mimi has taken her enjoyment of this plebeian pursuit one step further by becoming something of an authority on the subject. She's not only sampled everything from Nathan's famous to Munich weiss-würst, she has devised her own recipes for them. As a fellow hot-dog freak, I was happy to get a hold of some of these and the ones included here are Mimi's versions of New York's famous Sabrett-style hot dogs.

Makes 6 hot dogs on rolls with onions

2 medium onions, peeled
2 tablespoons vegetable oil
1–1½ tablespoons paprika
¼ teaspoon ground cumin
½ teaspoon salt
2–3 dashes pepper
½ cup water
6 long, thin hot dogs
6 hot dog rolls

1. Slice onions thinly into rings, or cut into vertical quarters and then slice lengthwise. The direction is not critical, but the latter is more authentic. Slices should be a little less than ¼ inch thick. Separate rings or vertical slices. Heat oil in a saucepan. Add onions and toss gently until all are coated with oil.

2. Toss in paprika, cumin, salt, and pepper. Cover and braise slowly over very low heat, stirring once in a while. Braise for about 10 minutes, but be sure onions do not brown. Add water as mixture becomes dry. Cover and braise for an additional 10 minutes, or until onions are tender, but a little firm, though not at all crisp. Taste; add additional seasoning, if you wish.

3. Prick hot-dog skins with a fork; drop into a pot of cold water and bring to a simmer. Simmer, uncovered, for about 10 minutes. Do not let water come to a rapid boil, and do not cover the pot, or the hot dogs will split.

4. Rolls can be toasted under the broiler, with or without a light coating of butter, but if you want to imitate the street-corner variety, just get them as cold and soggy as possible.

Note: The onions can be made hours in advance of a party, but if you intend to hold them for more than an hour, add an additional ¼ cup water when they have finished cooking, or before you reheat them. These onions are also delicious on hamburgers or steak sandwiches.

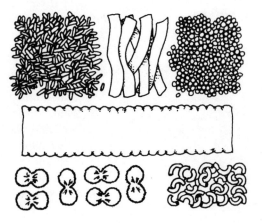

Italian Street Festa Sausages

This is Mimi's recipe for the Italian street festa sausages—those fat sausage-and-pepper combinations served on hero rolls. They are perfect for cooking on the outdoor grill.

Makes 1 serving

2 Italian pork sausages, sweet or hot
1 long, green, hot chili pepper or 2 strips sweet green pepper
1 individual-size hero loaf or roll

1. Run skewers through the length of sausages with whole hot pepper, or strips of sweet pepper between them.
2. Broil slowly over charcoal or wood fire, 4 to 6 inches from heat, turning frequently, allowing about 30 minutes total cooking time.
3. To cut cooking time, and to be sure pork is thoroughly cooked, sausages can be parboiled in advance. Prick skin in a few places with tines of a fork, so sausages don't burst their skins, and place in a skillet. Cover with water and bring slowly to a simmer. Do not cover pan. Poach gently for about 7 minutes. Dry surface on paper toweling and broil while hot.

4. Slip sausage and peppers off skewer onto a roll or a cut section of a long Italian bread.

Note: At street fairs, the sausages are broiled on sword-bladed skewers, as they will spin around on regular round skewers. Use the regular, round skewers and follow the instructions for threading to avoid this.

Fried Sausages with Peppers and Onions

This is a mixture Mimi Sheraton found at the 1975 New York State Fair in Syracuse. It's a gigantic, mouth-watering mess that looks almost impossible to tackle, says Mimi, but it's one any self-respecting hot-dog lover will find irresistible.

Makes 4 servings

3 tablespoons olive or vegetable oil
2 medium onions, peeled, thinly sliced, and separated into rings
3 Italian frying or banana peppers or 1 large green pepper, seeded and cut in thin vertical strips
1½ pounds Italian sausages, sweet or hot, preferably the thin rope of frying sausage

1 teaspoon salt
1 tablespoon leaf oregano, crumbled
4 individual hero loaves or 1 long Italian bread cut into 4 5-inch lengths
Pizzaiola Sauce (recipe follows)

1. Heat oil in a large skillet; gently sauté onions and peppers, stirring frequently. In about 10 minutes, onions and peppers should begin to wilt and become tender, and their edges should be faintly golden brown. Remove and reserve.
2. Prick sausages in several places with tines of a fork; add to skillet and brown slowly, rotating frequently so all sides brown, about 10 minutes. If you use rope sausage, brown in a coil, turning over, pancake style, to brown second side. Cut in 1½-inch pieces.
3. Return onions and peppers to pan and sprinkle with salt and oregano. Cover and braise over very low heat until sausages are done, about 10 additional minutes. Serve sausages with onions and peppers on hero loaves. Crushed hot red peppers can be sprinkled on top. To serve as at the New York State Fair, pour pizzaiola sauce over sausages after topping with peppers and onions.

Pizzaiola Sauce

Makes about 2 cups

2 tablespoons olive oil
2 cloves garlic, sliced
1 can (1 pound 1 ounce) Italian plum tomatoes, preferably packed with paste
½ small (6-ounce) can tomato paste, if none is in tomatoes
2 tablespoons leaf oregano, crumbled
1 teaspoon leaf basil, crumbled or 4 fresh basil leaves, chopped
½ teaspoon salt
¼ teaspoon pepper
Pinch of sugar

1. Heat oil and slowly sauté garlic until it is golden brown. Do not let it turn dark brown or black.
2. Drain tomatoes, reserving the liquid. Chop tomatoes coarsely and stir into oil and garlic. Simmer, covered, for about 15 minutes; add tomato paste beaten into 3 tablespoons of reserved tomato liquid.
3. Add oregano and basil, and season with salt, pepper, and sugar if needed. Simmer for 15 minutes, adding more tomato liquid if sauce is too thick, more paste if it is too thin. This will be enough sauce for 4 to 6 sausage hero sandwiches.

Real Texas Tacos

Tacos are folded tortilla shells, filled with seasoned ground meat, chicken, or beans, and topped with chopped lettuce, tomatoes, and cheese. In this recipe, brought directly from Texas by food writer Nika Hazelton, the tacos have an extra-zippy addition— Red Hot Pepper Sauce. You sprinkle this on top of the filling . . . carefully.

Makes 12 tacos

1 medium onion, chopped (½ cup)
1 clove garlic, crushed
2 tablespoons vegetable oil
1 pound ground beef
1 large tomato, peeled and chopped (1 cup)
1 teaspoon leaf oregano, crumbled
1 teaspoon salt
⅛ teaspoon pepper
1 9-ounce package frozen tortillas (12 per package)
Vegetable oil for frying
1 small head lettuce, shredded (about 2 cups)
8 ounces cheddar cheese, shredded (about 2 cups)
3 medium tomatoes, peeled and chopped
Red Hot Pepper Sauce (recipe follows)

1. In a large skillet sauté onion and garlic in 2 tablespoons oil until soft, about 5 minutes; add ground beef. Cook until brown. Add tomato, oregano, salt, and pepper. Cook, stirring frequently, for 10 minutes, or until heated through and sauce is thick.
2. Cook tortillas, following package directions. Heat about 1 inch of oil in a large skillet to 370 degrees on deep-fat thermometer. Drop tortillas into oil, 1 at a time. Using 2 forks, fold tortilla in half. Hold tortilla folded with tines of fork. Fry until tortilla holds its shape and is lightly browned and crisp, about 3 minutes. Drain on paper toweling.
3. Stuff 3 tablespoons beef filling, and some lettuce, cheese, and tomatoes into each taco. Add a few teaspoonfuls of red hot pepper sauce and garnish with onion rings, if you wish.

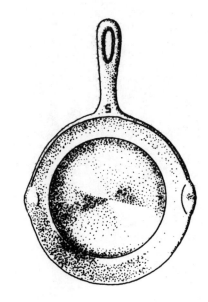

Red Hot Pepper Sauce

Makes 2½ cups

2 large tomatoes, peeled and chopped
1 medium onion, chopped (½ cup)
1 hot, green chili pepper (canned), seeded and chopped
2 tablespoons vegetable oil
¼ cup lemon juice
1 teaspoon salt
¼ teaspoon leaf oregano, crumbled
⅛ teaspoon pepper

1. Combine all ingredients in a medium-sized bowl. Store in refrigerator until serving time.
2. Spoon over hot tacos.

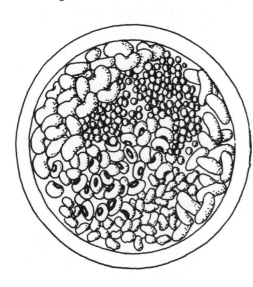

Brennan's Eggs Hussarde

Brennan's in New Orleans is the only restaurant I know that serves breakfast until 2:30 p.m.—but then all the dishes on their menu are good regardless of the time. This is one of them, and it's extremely popular with Brennan's clientele. The eggs are similar to eggs benedict because they're poached and served on English muffins with ham and hollandaise sauce. But the marchand de vin sauce also used in this recipe makes the dish truly unique. Try it for your next brunch.

Makes 4 servings

16 thin slices cooked ham (approximately 1 pound)
8 thick slices tomato
8 Holland rusks or 4 English muffins, split and toasted
8 soft poached eggs
Marchand de vin sauce (recipe follows)
Hollandaise sauce (recipe follows)

1. Arrange ham on broiler pan. Broil, 4 inches from heat, for about 3 minutes. Remove from broiler pan and keep warm. Arrange tomato slices on same broiler pan and broil for 2 minutes.

2. Place 2 ham slices on each rusk or English muffin and top with 2 tablespoons marchand de vin sauce. Arrange a tomato slice over sauce and center a poached egg on tomato slice.
3. Spoon hollandaise sauce over egg and garnish with parsley, if desired. Serve immediately.

1. Melt butter in a skillet. Sauté ham, onion, mushrooms, shallots, and garlic until onion begins to brown. Blend in flour, salt, pepper, and cayenne.
2. Cook, stirring constantly, until flour browns, about 7 minutes. Blend in beef broth and wine.
3. Heat sauce to boiling; reduce heat and simmer for 35 minutes to blend flavors.

Note: This sauce can be made the day before and stored in the refrigerator until it is ready to heat and spoon over the ham. Any extra suace will store for several days in the refrigerator, to be used in soups and stew gravies.

Marchand de Vin Sauce

Makes 2 cups

4 tablespoons (½ stick) butter
½ cup finely minced cooked ham
½ cup finely chopped onion (1 medium)
⅓ cup finely chopped raw mushrooms
⅓ cup finely chopped shallots
1 tablespoon minced garlic
2 tablespoons flour
½ teaspoon salt
⅛ teaspoon pepper
Dash of cayenne
¾ cup canned, condensed beef broth
½ cup dry red wine

Hollandaise Sauce

Makes about 1 cup

4 egg yolks
2 tablespoons lemon juice
½ pound (2 sticks) butter
¼ teaspoon salt
Dash of white pepper

1. Cut each stick of butter into 8 pieces.
2. Beat egg yolks with a wooden spoon in top of a double boiler until smooth; blend in lemon juice. Place over simmering, *not boiling*, water.
3. Add butter, 1 piece at a time, stirring constantly, until all butter has been added and sauce has thickened. Season with salt and pepper. Remove top of double boiler from water.

Note: Sauce can be made ahead of time and kept warm over simmering water. If sauce should separate, beat in a few drops of boiling water with a wooden spoon until sauce is smooth.

Lea Rabin's Blintzes

When a staff writer at Family Circle *was assigned to do a story on Jewish holiday cooking, she turned to Lea Rabin in Washington. Mrs. Rabin, wife of Israel's former ambassador to the United States, has a reputation as an imaginative and innovative cook, and she is an articulate student of Israel's history. This is one of the recipes Mrs. Rabin passed along to us, and it's a dish she says is served during Purim, a festive Jewish holiday celebrated in early spring. It's excellent and can be served either as a light luncheon dish or a dessert.*

Makes 24 blintzes

BATTER
4 eggs
2 cups sifted all-purpose flour
1 cup milk
1 cup water
4 tablespoons (½ stick) butter, melted

FILLING
2 packages (7½ ounces each) farmer cheese
2 packages (8 ounces each) cream cheese
4 eggs
1 teaspoon salt
6 tablespoons (¾ stick) butter

1. Beat eggs just until blended in a large bowl; sift flour over eggs and beat in just until smooth. Stir in milk, water, and butter. Chill for 1 hour. While batter chills, prepare filling.
2. Combine farmer cheese, cream cheese, eggs, and salt in large bowl of electric mixer. Beat at medium speed for about 3 minutes, or just until smooth.
3. Heat a 7-inch skillet slowly over medium heat. Grease lightly with a little butter.
4. Measure chilled batter, a scant ¼ cup at a time, into skillet, tilting to cover bottom completely.
5. Cook 1 to 2 minutes, or until top is set and underside is golden; turn over and cook lightly on other side. Remove to a plate. Repeat with remaining batter, to make 24 blintzes. Stack on plate.
6. Place 3 tablespoons of the cheese filling on center of the browned side of each blintz. Roll up, jelly-roll style.
7. Melt remaining butter in a large skillet. Brown blintzes, turning to brown all over. Keep warm until all blintzes have been browned. Serve hot with sour cream and applesauce or strawberries.

Burt Reynolds' Parmesan Garlic Toast

Maybe you find it hard to imagine Burt Reynolds behind a stove. Nonetheless, he does enjoy cooking at least once in a while. And when the mood strikes, there's one thing you can be sure of—the food will have plenty of garlic in it. Burt says this is probably a throwback to his Italian heritage, but whatever the reason, he makes a wicked garlic bread.

Makes 8 slices

8 tablespoons (1 stick) soft butter
½ cup grated parmesan cheese
1 clove garlic, crushed
8 slices French sourdough bread or Italian bread

1. Combine butter, cheese, and garlic.
2. Pile mixture high on 8 thick slices of bread (or hard sliced rolls, or, in a pinch, use English muffins).
3. Place the slices on a double thickness of aluminum foil. Bake in hot oven, 400 degrees, for 10 minutes. Garnish with a dash of paprika.

Saratoga Potato Chips

Mimi Sheraton is an inquisitive cook, as I discovered recently when she said, "Well, do you know where potato chips were first made?" Of course, I didn't. Apparently, this all-American specialty was the nineteenth-century invention of a chef at the Moon's Lake House in Saratoga Springs, New York, when it was a fashionable resort. And it was from that point on that they eventually grew to become one of America's favorite snacks. Mimi gave me a recipe for making potato chips at home, just like the originals. They're great!

Makes 4 servings

3 large, dry baking potatoes
  Vegetable oil
  Salt

1. Pare potatoes and slice, crosswise, into rounds that are tissue-thin and uniform. (To do this, use a cutter known as a mandolin, available in department store cookware sections, or a vegetable slicer that works by hand or attaches to an electric mixer.)
2. Soak sliced potatoes in several changes of very cold water for 2 hours, adding ice cubes to the last change of water. Turn potatoes onto a towel and dry each slice very thoroughly on both sides.
3. Fill a deep-fat fryer with vegetable oil to a depth of 3 inches. Heat to 375 degrees on a deep-fat thermometer, or until a 1-inch cube of bread turns golden in 60 seconds.
4. Place a few potato slices at a time in frying basket; lower into hot fat, shaking basket to avoid sticking. Fry for 4 to 5 minutes, or until golden-brown.
5. Drain on paper towels; continue frying remaining potato slices, being sure that fat remains at a constant 375 degrees. Sprinkle with salt just before serving.

Note: These are best warm and are wonderful accompaniments to steak and hamburgers. Do not expect them to stay crisp as long as the commercial variations, which are treated with special crispers.

Best of the Best Desserts

Ernie's French Apple Tart
Jane O'Keefe's Homemade Apple Pie
Alma McGraw's Grated Apple Pie with
    Streusel Topping
Mary Rohrer's Shoo-Fly Pie
Mrs. Delpha Zietz's Pecan Pie
Best of the Best Lemon Meringue Pie
John Clancy's Cheesecake
Upside-Down Orange Cheesecake
Maxwell's Plum Black Forest Chocolate Cake
My Favorite Chocolate Fudge Cake
Helen McCully's Rich Strawberry Shortcake
Helen Feingold's Chocolate-Dipped Strawberries
Lutece's Miniature Orange Soufflés
Marie Walsh's Scientifically Super Brownies
Mimi Sheraton's Double Chocolate Pudding
Nika Hazelton's Rødgrød
Fauchon's Chocolate Mousse
Ann Seranne's Foolproof Crème Brûlée
The Best-Ever Chocolate Chip Cookies
My Mother's Mocha Nut Butter Cookies
Emily's Walnut Crescents

Ernie's French Apple Tart

I like this apple tart because it's so simple to make. The apples are placed in a circular pattern on a bottom crust and, instead of a top crust, they're covered with a sprinkling of sugar and glazed with apple jelly. It's a particularly delicious combination and one that eliminates frustrations for people who are clumsy pastry-makers as I often am.

Another thing I like is to visit Ernie's Restaurant in San Francisco, where the recipe was first created. Owners Victor and Roland Gotti first served the tart at a dinner for Paul Bocuse, a famous French chef, and it is now just one of the many interesting French specialties offered on their menu. The restaurant itself is a treat. It's an opulent Victorian setting complete with a mahogany and stained-glass bar that came to California over a century ago on a sailing ship via Cape Horn. The next time you're in San Francisco, pay the Gottis a visit. In the meantime, try their recipe for French apple tart.

Makes 8 servings

Pâte Sucrée (recipe follows)
10 cups apples, peeled, quartered, cored, and sliced (approximately 8–10 apples)
¾ cup sugar
¼ cup water
1 teaspoon lemon juice
4 tablespoons apple jelly

1. Make the pâté sucrée and chill.
2. Place 6 cups of the apples in a large saucepan with ½ cup sugar and the water. Cook, covered, over low heat for 20 minutes, or until soft, stirring occasionally. Beat with a wooden spoon until sauce is smooth. Cool.
3. Roll pastry on lightly floured surface to a 12-inch round. Fit into a 10-inch fluted tart pan with loose bottom (or use a 10-inch pie plate). Press edge firmly against side of pan. Chill for 30 minutes. Prick bottom of pastry shell with a fork.
4. Bake in moderate oven, 350 degrees, for 10 minutes. Spread apple sauce over bottom. Toss remaining 4 cups apple with lemon juice. Starting from outside edge, arrange slices over apple sauce, overlapping in circular pattern. Sprinkle with remaining ¼ cup sugar.

5. Bake in moderate oven, 350 degrees, for 35 minutes, or until apples are done. Place briefly under broiler with top of tart 3 to 4 inches from heat until lightly browned. Remove to wire rack to cool.
6. Melt apple jelly in small saucepan over low heat. Brush over top of apples to glaze. Serve with whipped cream, if desired.

Pâte Sucrée

1½ cups unsifted flour
¼ cup sugar
8 tablespoons 1 (stick) butter
1 egg
2 egg yolks
½ teaspoon vanilla

1. Mix flour and sugar together in a medium-sized bowl; cut in butter with pastry blender until mixture is crumbly.
2. Add egg, egg yolks, and vanilla; mix lightly with a fork just until pastry holds together. Knead a few times; chill at least 1 hour.

Jane O'Keefe's Homemade Apple Pie

As a professional home economist and director of Family Circle's Test Kitchen, *Jane O'Keefe has a sophisticated knowledge of food. She knows what's good and how to make the simplest or most complicated meal beautifully appealing. She also believes, after trying dozens of recipes, that her own mother's apple pie is one of the best. And I agree.*

This apple pie has a wonderful homemade quality. It doesn't involve any fancy pastry cutting—just simple V-shaped vents in the top crust to let out steam as the apples cook. It doesn't even require special cooking apples. Jane uses Rome Beauties, but almost any kind can be substituted. And the pie is really full—with no little space between the top crust and the apples. Cooled for an hour and served plain or with ice cream or cheese, it's unbeatable.

Makes 1 9-inch pie

2½ pounds apples, pared, quar-
    tered, cored, and thinly sliced
    (8 cups)
⅓ cup firmly packed light brown
    sugar
⅓ cup granulated sugar
1 tablespoon cornstarch or 2 table-
    spoons flour
1 teaspoon ground cinnamon
¼ teaspoon ground nutmeg
¼ teaspoon salt
1 package piecrust mix
2 tablespoons butter
    Water or milk
    Sugar for sprinkling

1. Place apples in large bowl; mix
   sugars, cornstarch, cinnamon,
   nutmeg, and salt in a small
   bowl. Sprinkle over apples; toss
   gently to mix. Let stand until
   a little juice forms, about 10
   minutes.
2. Meanwhile, prepare piecrust
   mix, following package directions. Roll out ½ of dough to a
   12-inch round on a lightly
   floured surface; fit into a 9-inch
   pie plate. Trim overhang to ½
   inch.
3. Roll out remaining pastry for
   top to a 12-inch round. Fold
   into quarters; make 3 slits near
   center in each of folded edges
   for steam to escape. Pile apple
   mixture into pastry; dot with
   butter. Moisten edge of bottom
   pastry with water. Place folded

pastry on apples so point is on
center; unfold. Trim overhang
to 1 inch; turn edges under and
press together to seal. Pinch to
make stand-up edge; flute or
make your favorite edging.
4. For a crispy-sugary top, brush
   top of pastry with a little water
   or milk and sprinkle lightly
   with sugar.
5. Bake pie in hot oven, 425 degrees, for 40 minutes, or until
   juices bubble through slits and
   apples are tender. If edge is
   browning too fast, cover with
   a narrow strip of foil. Serve
   warm with vanilla ice cream or
   chunks of cheddar cheese.

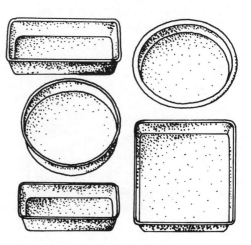

Alma McGraw's Grated Apple Pie with Streusel Topping

"When told that she has a reputation for being one of the best cooks in Finney County, Kansas, Alma Mc-Graw blushes." But, says Jean Anderson who reported on Mrs. Mc-Graw for Family Circle's *grass-roots cooking series, it's true. And, according to her friends and neighbors, one of Mrs. McGraw's finest recipes is this one for apple pie—which she developed herself. It's a recipe from heartland America that will reach the heart of all apple-pie lovers.*

Makes 1 10-inch pie

6 medium Jonathan or McIntosh apples, firm and crisp
½ cup sugar
½ cup plus 2 tablespoons unsifted all-purpose flour
1 tablespoon lemon juice
¼ teaspoon ground cinnamon
⅛ teaspoon salt
½ cup firmly packed light brown sugar
⅛ teaspoon salt
2 tablespoons butter, softened to room temperature
1 10-inch unbaked pie shell (use your own recipe, or try Alma McGraw's Egg and Vinegar Piecrust; recipe follows)

1. Quarter, core, and coarsely grate apples. (Do not peel them.) Mix apples thoroughly with sugar, 2 tablespoons flour, lemon juice, cinnamon, and salt.
2. Combine brown sugar, ½ cup flour, and salt, pressing out any lumps of sugar. Using your hands, rub in the butter until mixture is crumbly. This is the streusel topping.
3. Spoon apple mixture into unbaked pie shell, then scatter sugar mixture (streusel) evenly over the top.
4. Bake in a hot oven, 400 degrees, for 10 minutes; lower temperature to moderate, 375 degrees, and bake for 25 to 30 minutes

longer, until filling is bubbly and streusel topping is dappled with brown.

5. Remove pie from oven and let cool for 20 to 25 minutes before cutting.

Egg and Vinegar Piecrust

Makes 3 8-inch or 2 9-inch pie shells, or 1 9- or 10-inch double-crust pie

  1 **cup chilled vegetable shortening**
3¼ **cups sifted all-purpose flour**
 ¾ **teaspoon salt**
  1 **egg, beaten until frothy, then mixed with enough cold water to make ¾ cup**
  1 **teaspoon cider vinegar**

1. Cut shortening into flour and salt with a pastry blender until it is the texture of coarse crumbs. Combine egg–water mixture with vinegar and add to the flour mixture a little at a time, mixing briskly with a fork until pastry just holds together. (Do not overmix or pastry will be tough.)

2. Divide pastry into 3 equal parts (for 8-inch pie shells) or 2 equal parts (for 9- or 10-inch

pie shells, or a 9-inch or 10-inch double-crust pie).

3. Roll pastry on a lightly floured pastry cloth with a lightly floured, stockinette-covered rolling pin into a circle 3 inches larger than the pie pan. Place rolling pin across center of pastry circle, lop half of pastry over rolling pin, and ease into pie pan. Fit pastry snugly into pan and trim overhang so that it is 1 inch larger than the pie pan all around. Roll under and crimp, making a decorative edge. Pie shell is ready to fill and bake (or to wrap in plastic food wrap and freeze).

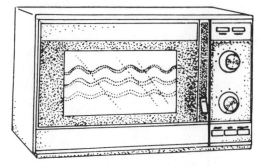

Mary Rohrer's Shoo-Fly Pie

When food writer Jean Anderson interviewed Mrs. Mary Rohrer of Manheim, Pennsylvania, for an article on Pennsylvania-Dutch cooking, she discovered a gourmet chef in housewife's clothing. And, after more than 50 years of cooking in her farmhouse kitchen, not only does Mrs. Rohrer know what she's doing, but she still enjoys it. Her specialties include a wide variety of popular local fare. Among them is shoo-fly pie, which she prepares in a half dozen ways. But this recipe is the one she likes best, as I expect you will. It's known as a "wet-bottomed" pie (many shoo-fly pies are very dry, almost cake-like), and its ingredients include both molasses and dark corn syrup, which accounts for its rich but not overly sweet flavor.

Makes 1 9-inch pie

¾ cup dark corn syrup
¼ cup molasses
1 cup boiling water
1 teaspoon baking soda
1 egg, lightly beaten
1 cup sifted all-purpose flour
2 tablespoons shortening or lard
⅔ cup firmly packed dark brown sugar
1 unbaked 9-inch pie shell

1. In a medium-size mixing bowl, combine corn syrup, molasses, and water; stir in baking soda. Beat a little molasses mixture into the egg, then stir back into mixing bowl.
2. With a pastry blender, mix together flour, shortening or lard, and sugar until it is the texture of coarse crumbs. Mix 1 cup of this crumb mixture into the molasses mixture. Pour into unbaked pie shell. Scatter remaining crumbs on top.
3. Bake in a hot oven, 400 degrees, for 25 minutes, or until crust is lightly browned and filling is puffy. Remove from oven and let cool to room temperature before cutting.

Mrs. Delpha Zietz's Pecan Pie

Texans have a knack for making everything seem bigger than life. But often what may sound like boasting to an outsider is, in fact, true. For instance, if a native tells you about the state's large pecan crop, don't snicker. This food is one of their largest agricultural products and an extremely popular one with Texan cooks. So if you don't have a recipe for pecan pie, ask anyone from Texas; or try this one from Mrs. Delpha Zietz of San Antonio. It's her favorite, and it's big in my book too.

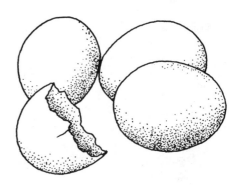

Makes 1 8-inch pie

3 eggs
1 cup sugar
½ cup light corn syrup
   Dash of salt
1 teaspoon vanilla
1 cup chopped pecans
1 8-inch unbaked pastry shell
   Pecan halves for garnish

1. Beat eggs until frothy in a medium-size bowl. Add sugar, corn syrup, salt, vanilla, and pecans. Mix well. Pour into pastry shell. Arrange pecans on top.
2. Bake in hot oven, 400 degrees, for 10 minutes; lower temperature to 350 degrees. Bake for 30 minutes longer, or until almost firm in center. Cool.

Best of the Best Lemon Meringue Pie

There's nothing mysterious about making lemon meringue pie—except when the filling gets runny for what seems like an unexplained reason. Since this has happened to me, I asked Jane O'Keefe about it. She offered the following explanation and a solution. "The problem," Jane noted, "is probably due to that extra heat on the cold filling when the meringue top browns in the oven. To guarantee against this, bake the meringue separately in little puffs and then place them on top of the chilled lemon filling." The method works—and so does the recipe.

Makes 1 9-inch single-crust pie

½ package piecrust mix
2 cups sugar
½ cup cornstarch
¼ teaspoon salt
2½ cups water
4 eggs, separated
3 tablespoons butter
1 tablespoon grated lemon rind
½ cup lemon juice
¼ teaspoon cream of tartar

1. Prepare piecrust mix; fit into a 9-inch pie plate making a high stand-up edge. Prick shell all over with a fork.
2. Bake in a very hot oven, 450 degrees, for 5 minutes. If bubbles have formed in shell, prick again. Bake for another 10 minutes, or until pastry is golden brown. Cool completely in pie plate on wire rack.
3. Combine 1½ cups sugar, cornstarch, and salt in a large saucepan; gradually add the water, stirring with a wooden spoon.
4. Cook over medium heat, stirring constantly, until mixture thickens and bubbles. Cook for 1 minute and remove from heat.
5. Beat egg yolks slightly in a small bowl; slowly blend in about ½ cup of the hot cornstarch mixture; stir back into remaining mixture in saucepan. Cook over low heat, stirring constantly, for 2 minutes; re-move from heat. (Do not over-cook.)
6. Stir in butter, lemon rind, and lemon juice; pour into cooled pastry shell. Press a piece of plastic wrap directly on filling to prevent formation of a skin. (Remove before topping pie.) Refrigerate for at least 4 hours.
7. Beat egg whites with cream of tartar in a medium-size bowl until foamy-white. Slowly add remaining ½ cup sugar, a table-spoon at a time, beating at high speed until the meringue forms firm peaks.
8. Grease and lightly flour a small cooky sheet. Shape meringue into 6 to 8 small mounds on cooky sheet, swirling with the back of a teaspoon to form peaks.
9. Bake in moderate oven, 350 degrees, for 15 minutes or until meringues are golden. Cool on cooky sheet. When the puffs are cool, carefully place on chilled pie with a small spatula.

Note: This recipe was developed to fill a 9-inch-wide and 1¼-inch-deep pie plate (4 cups level to rim). For a shallower plate, fill baked pastry only to fluted rim and save remainder to use as a filling for cake layers.

John Clancy's Cheesecake

New Yorkers pride themselves on being authorities on cheesecake, and it's not beyond the realm of possibility to hear two otherwise intelligent adults arguing the merits of one bakery's cheesecake over another's. I know one man who, insisting that the only real cheesecake is made by a bakery somewhere in Brooklyn, periodically takes off in that direction on the subway.

I guess this mania is understandable because I looked for a long time, too, before finding this recipe by chef John Clancy. It has a light, lemony flavor that accentuates the purity of the cream cheese, and it's just sweet enough to leave the emphasis on the richness that is the very reason for eating cheesecake. The texture is great too—firm and even, from top to bottom, without being too solid. And it's a recipe that will stand you in good stead the next time someone wants to talk about cheesecake!

Makes 1 9-inch cake

1½ cups graham-cracker crumbs
3 tablespoons sugar
½ teaspoon ground cinnamon
4 tablespoons (½ stick) unsalted butter, melted
3 packages (8 ounces each) cream cheese, room temperature
1¼ cups sugar
6 eggs, separated
1 cup (1 pint) dairy sour cream
⅓ cup all-purpose flour
2 teaspoons vanilla
Grated rind of 1 lemon
Juice of ½ lemon

1. Generously grease a 9-by-3-inch springform pan with butter. Place pan in center of a 12-inch square of aluminum foil; press foil up around sides of pan.
2. Combine the graham-cracker crumbs, 3 tablespoons sugar, cinnamon, and melted butter in a small bowl until well-blended. Press ¾ cup of crumb mixture into bottom and sides of pan. Chill prepared pan while making filling. (Reserve remaining crumb mixture for topping.)
3. With electric mixer on low speed or with a wooden spoon, beat cream cheese in a large bowl until soft. Gradually beat in 1¼ cups sugar until light and fluffy.

4. Beat in egg yolks, one at a time, until well-blended. Stir in sour cream, flour, vanilla, lemon rind, and lemon juice until smooth.
5. Beat egg whites until they hold stiff peaks. Fold whites into cheese mixture, soufflé-fashion, until well blended. Pour into prepared pan.
6. Bake in moderate oven, 350 degrees, for 1 hour and 15 minutes, or until top is golden; turn off oven heat and allow cake to cool in oven for 1 hour.
7. Remove cake from oven and allow to cool on a wire rack at room temperature. Sprinkle remaining crumbs on top.
8. Chill overnight before serving. Dust with confectioners sugar just before serving.

Upside-Down Orange Cheesecake

This is a beautiful cheesecake for three reasons. It doesn't require any baking and it tastes and looks great. The orange slices used for the topping are combined with gelatin, placed in a circular pattern on the bottom of the pan, and covered with the cottage cheese-sour cream filling. Then when you serve the cake, simply flip it over, remove the pan, and admire your work.

Makes 10 servings

> 2 envelopes unflavored gelatin
> 1½ cups orange juice
> 1 cup sugar
> 1 orange, thinly sliced
> 3 eggs, separated
> 1 tablespoon grated orange rind
> 2 tablespoons orange flavored liqueur
> 1½ pounds (3 cups) cottage cheese
> ½ cup dairy sour cream
> 1 cup vanilla wafer crumbs
> ½ teaspoon ground cinnamon
> 3 tablespoons butter, melted

1. Soften 1 teaspoon gelatin in ¾ cup orange juice for 5 minutes; stir in ½ cup sugar. Heat, stirring constantly, over medium heat, until gelatin melts. Chill until syrupy-thick.

2. Arrange orange slices in concentric circles in a 9-by-9-by-2-inch pan. Pour syrupy orange juice over. Chill.

3. In a small pan soften remaining gelatin in remaining juice for 5 minutes. Heat, stirring constantly, until just below boiling point. Beat egg yolks slightly in a small bowl. Slowly add half the hot gelatin mixture; stir back into pan. Cook, stirring constantly, until mixture thickens slightly. (Do not allow to boil.) Remove from heat; stir in orange rind and orange liqueur.

4. Combine half the cottage cheese, half the sour cream, and half the gelatin mixture in electric blender. Whirl at high speed until smooth and completely blended. Pour into large bowl. Repeat with remaining cheese, sour cream, and gelatin mixture. Chill, stirring often, until mixture mounds slightly when spooned.

5. Beat egg whites in a small bowl until foamy-white and double in volume. Beat in remaining sugar, 1 tablespoon at a time, until meringue stands in firm peaks. Fold meringue into cottage cheese mixture. Pour over orange layer in pan. Chill at least 4 hours, or until firm.

6. Combine crumbs with cinnamon in small bowl; blend in butter. Spread over top of cheesecake and press down firmly with hands. Chill briefly to set crumb layer.

7. Loosen cake around edge with a small spatula; dip pan quickly in and out of hot water. Place serving plate over pan, turn upside down. Shake pan gently to release cake; lift off pan. Keep refrigerated until serving time.

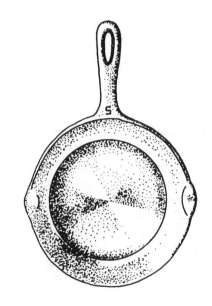

Maxwell's Plum Black Forest Chocolate Cake

Dinner at Maxwell's Plum in New York is always an occasion to remember, particularly when it ends with Black Forest chocolate cake. Traditionally made in three very thin, deep-dark chocolate layers, the cake is covered with a mountain of fluffy-light, chocolate whipped cream. And it's impossible for any self-respecting chocolate lover to resist ordering it. I've tried.

Makes 1 9-inch cake

⅔ cup sifted cake flour (sift before measuring)
2 tablespoons cornstarch
2 tablespoons unsweetened cocoa powder (*not* a mix)
2 tablespoons butter
5 large eggs
⅓ cup sugar
3 tablespoons kirsch (cherry brandy)
8 cups Black Forest cream (recipe follows)
Chocolate curls (recipe follows)
3 bottles (1¾ ounces each) chocolate sprinkles

1. Prepare a 9-inch springform pan by buttering well and sprinkling with flour, tapping out excess.
2. Sift flour, cornstarch, and cocoa powder together 3 times to make mixture very light.
3. Heat butter in a small metal cup until hot, but not bubbling; keep warm, while beating eggs.
4. Break eggs into a deep, 3-quart heatproof bowl; stir in sugar. Place bowl in a large skillet half filled with hot, but not boiling water.
5. Place skillet over low heat and warm egg mixture, stirring constantly, until mixture is warmed to 98 degrees (body temperature), about 3 minutes. (Stick your finger into mixture; if it feels comfortable, it's right.) Remove bowl from water.
6. Place electric mixer beaters into bowl. If beaters are not covered with egg mixture, tilt bowl until beaters are as covered as possible. Beat at high speed, turning both beaters and bowl, for 5 minutes. (The mixture should be so thick and velvety that the pattern of

beaters through the mixture looks like the wavy edge of Christmas ribbon candy. This is a whole egg meringue. It should be firm and velvety with all the very large air bubbles beaten away. You should be able to turn the bowl upside down without the mixture falling out.)

7. Fold flour mixture very gently into eggs with a wire whip until well blended. Fold in hot butter with wire whip, just until blended; pour into prepared pan. Place pan on rack in center of oven.

8. Bake in moderate oven, 350 degrees, for 30 minutes, or until center springs back when lightly pressed with fingertip.

9. Cool cake in pan on wire rack for 15 minutes. Run a thin-bladed knife around edge of pan to loosen cake; invert onto wire rack and cool completely. (Cake will only be about 1½ inches high, but very rich.)

10. Slice cake, crosswise, into 3 ½-inch layers with a long serrated slicing knife. Sprinkle kirsch over each layer.

11. Place one layer on cake stand; spread with a generous coating of Black Forest cream. Top with second layer; spread with Black Forest cream. Top with last layer and spread remaining Black Forest cream over top and side to make a thickly coated cake. Arrange chocolate curls on top and coat side with chocolate sprinkles. Chill at least 4 hours before serving.

Black Forest Cream

Makes 8 cups, or enough to fill and frost 1 9-inch cake

4 cups heavy cream (1 quart)
½ cup confectioners sugar
12 squares semisweet chocolate squares

1. Beat cream and sugar in a large, deep bowl with an electric mixer until stiff; refrigerate.

2. Melt chocolate in top of a double boiler over simmering water. Add 2 cups whipped cream to melted chocolate; keep over water and fold in with a wire whip, just until chocolate and cream are blended. Pour chocolate mixture over whipped cream.

3. Fold lightly and slowly with a wire whip until mixture is well blended.

Chocolate Curls

4 squares semisweet chocolate

1. Melt chocolate in top of a double boiler over simmering water, stirring several times. Spread into a 4-inch square on a cold cooky sheet.
2. Refrigerate for 15 minutes, or just until chocolate sets. Pull a thin-bladed, long knife across chocolate, letting the soft chocolate curl up in front of the knife. (It takes a little practice, so count on a few to be less than perfect; put these on the cake first. Save the prettiest curls for the top.)

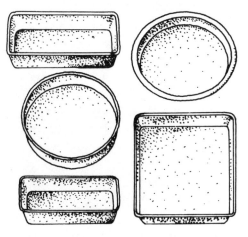

My Favorite Chocolate Fudge Cake

Finding the best recipe for chocolate cake was a tall order, as our food department at Family Circle *discovered when they tried to pick a favorite from the more than twenty recipes they had developed. But after many very pleasant samplings, this was the one they selected. It's the cake I have whenever a chocolate fit strikes.*

It's easy to prepare and requires little in the way of pampering, except that it's best to work quickly once you've added the baking soda. This is important because baking soda is a fast-acting ingredient and shouldn't sit too long before it reaches the heat of the oven. This also means you should have the oven preheated to 350 degrees. Other than that, I can only advise you to sit back and slice off a second helping.

Makes 12 servings

3 squares unsweetened chocolate
2¼ cups sifted cake flour
2 teaspoons baking soda
½ teaspoon salt
8 tablespoons (1 stick) butter
2¼ cups firmly packed light brown sugar

3 eggs
1½ teaspoons vanilla
1 cup dairy sour cream
1 cup boiling water
Chocolate Fudge Frosting (recipe follows)

1. Melt chocolate in a small bowl over hot but not boiling water; cool.
2. Grease and flour two 9-by-1½-inch layer cake pans; tap out excess flour.
3. Sift flour, baking soda, and salt onto wax paper.
4. Beat butter until soft in large bowl. Add brown sugar and eggs; beat with mixer for 5 minutes at high speed until light and fluffy. Beat in vanilla and cooled, melted chocolate.
5. Stir in dry ingredients alternately with sour cream, beating well with a wooden spoon after each addition until batter is smooth. Stir in boiling water. (Batter will be thin.) Pour at once into prepared pans.
6. Bake in moderate oven, 350 degrees, for 35 minutes, or until centers spring back when lightly pressed with fingertip.
7. Cool layers in pans on wire rack for 10 minutes; loosen around edges with a small knife or spatula. Turn out onto wire racks; cool completely.
8. Make chocolate fudge frosting. Put one cake layer on a serving plate; spread with about ¼ of the frosting. Add second layer; spread remainder on side and top of cake, making swirls with spatula.

Chocolate Fudge Frosting

Makes enough to fill and frost 2 9-inch layers

4 squares unsweetened chocolate
8 tablespoons (1 stick) butter
1 pound confectioners sugar
½ cup milk
2 teaspoons vanilla

1. Combine chocolate and butter in small, heavy saucepan. Place over low heat, just until melted. Remove from heat.
2. Combine confectioners sugar, milk, and vanilla in medium-size bowl; stir until smooth. Add chocolate mixture. Set bowl in pan of ice and water; beat with wooden spoon until frosting is thick enough to spread and hold its shape.

Helen McCully's Rich Strawberry Shortcake

In making this cake you'll understand why Helen McCully has a reputation as a marvelous hostess. It's the kind of dessert that makes one feel right at home. Helen's recipe also shows that even a familiar favorite can seem excitingly new when it's beautifully prepared and presented. And if anyone can resist strawberry shortcake, it's definitely not me.

Makes 8 servings

2 cups all-purpose flour
¼ cup sugar
3 tablespoons double-acting baking powder
½ teaspoon salt
Few grains ground nutmeg
4 tablespoons (½ stick) butter, cut into 4 pieces
2 egg yolks, slightly beaten
⅓ cup cold milk
2 pints fresh strawberries, washed, hulled, and sliced
Sugar
1 cup heavy cream, whipped

1. Thoroughly grease an 8-inch round cake pan and set aside.
2. Sift flour, sugar, baking powder, salt, and nutmeg together in a large bowl. Work or cut in the butter with two knives or a pastry blender until the mixture looks mealy. Add egg yolks and milk; stir until all floury particles are mixed in, but do not attempt to beat the batter smooth.
3. Spoon batter into the prepared pan and smooth the top with a metal spatula. Bake in a hot oven, 450 degrees, for 12 minutes, or until a toothpick inserted in the center comes out clean. Turn out on a cake rack to cool.
4. While cake is baking, sweeten strawberries with granulated sugar to taste.
5. Cut the cake in half, crosswise. Place one layer on a serving platter. Cover with half the strawberries. Add the second cake layer, top with remaining strawberries and finish the whole beautiful shortcake with whipped cream.

Helen Feingold's Chocolate-Dipped Strawberries

How can you go wrong with a dessert called chocolate-dipped strawberries? Well, you can't, as you'll discover when you try this recipe Helen Feingold devised. It looks impressive, but it's particularly easy because there are only three ingredients to worry about, which makes it a really appealing company dessert.

Makes about 48

1 quart large firm strawberries
1 8-ounce package semi-sweet chocolate (do not use chocolate chips), coarsely chopped
¼ cup vegetable shortening

1. Wash strawberries (leave hulls on); dry completely on paper toweling.
2. Put chocolate and vegetable shortening in top of a double boiler. Place over hot, not boiling, water and stir until chocolate is melted and smooth. (Do not allow any water to get into the chocolate as this causes it to lump.)
3. Holding the strawberries by the hulls, dip them into melted chocolate until they are ¾

covered. Continue holding them over the chocolate until excess chocolate drains off, then place on a cookie sheet covered with wax paper. Chill until chocolate hardens.

Note: These strawberries should be prepared only a few hours in advance. Also, be sure to keep chocolate over the hot water while dipping all the strawberries. If chocolate becomes to shallow to dip, spoon up by tablespoonfuls and roll strawberries around to coat evenly.

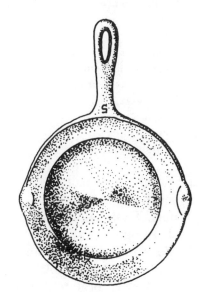

Lutece's Miniature Orange Soufflés

For haute cuisine, impeccable service, and a pristine setting, New York's Lutece is hard to surpass. It's the epitome of a fine French restaurant and a dining experience everyone should indulge in at least once in a while. These tiny soufflés will give you an idea of what pure pleasure their beautiful desserts are.

Makes 6 servings

> 4 tablespoons (½ stick) unsalted butter
> ½ cup all-purpose flour
> ⅓ cup plus 1½ tablespoons sugar
> 1½ cups milk, scalded
> 2 large navel oranges
> 5 egg yolks
> 2 tablespoons Grand Marnier
> 6 egg whites
> Confectioners sugar

1. Butter 8 small, individual soufflé dishes or 6 slightly larger ones. Dust lightly with sugar; shake out excess.
2. Melt butter in a saucepan. Blend in flour; cook, stirring constantly, for 1 to 2 minutes. Cool slightly (this is called a roux).
3. Combine sugar and milk; stir to dissolve. Whisk milk mixture rapidly into the roux until smooth. Cook, stirring constantly, until mixture thickens and comes to a boil. Remove from heat.
4. Grate rind from oranges; then peel and section.
5. Whisk egg yolks, grated orange rind, and Grand Marnier into hot mixture. Beat egg whites until stiff but not dry; fold into hot mixture.
6. Fill prepared soufflé dishes ⅓ full with soufflé mixture. Divide orange sections among the dishes. Add enough soufflé mixture to ¾ fill each dish. Smooth surfaces.
7. Bake in moderate oven, 375 degrees, for 18 minutes, or until soufflés are puffed and golden brown. Sprinkle tops with confectioners sugar and *serve at once*, while puffed and perfect. Any extra soufflé mixture can be warmed in a double boiler over hot, not boiling, water, thinned down with orange juice, or Grand Marnier, and served as a sauce.

Note: The same mixture can, of course, be baked in a single large soufflé dish (filled ¾ full). Bake at 325 degrees for 20 minutes, increase oven temperature to 350 degrees, and bake for 10 minutes longer, or until soufflé is well-puffed and golden brown.

Marie Walsh's Scientifically Super Brownies

If anyone ever doubts that cooking is a science as well as an art, I would recommend they talk with Marie Walsh. Marie, as I noted earlier on, is editor of Family Circle's Great Ideas *book series. In addition, she is a home economics wiz. She can tell you whether a recipe will work by glancing at it, what ingredients won't go together, as well as what to do if you "wreck the rice."*

So when I asked her for what she considered a foolproof, delicious recipe for brownies, I was confident in what I'd get.

Makes 16 brownies

2 squares unsweetened chocolate
8 tablespoons (1 stick) butter
2 eggs
1 cup sugar
1 teaspoon vanilla
½ cup sifted all-purpose flour
⅛ teaspoon salt
¾ cup chopped walnuts

1. Melt chocolate and butter in a small saucepan over low heat; cool.
2. Beat eggs in a small bowl with electric mixer; gradually beat in sugar until mixture is fluffy and thick. Stir in chocolate mixture and vanilla.
3. Fold in flour and salt until well blended; stir in walnuts. Spread evenly in an 8-by-8-by-2-inch greased baking pan.
4. Bake in moderate oven, 350 degrees, for 30 minutes, or until shiny and firm on top. Cool in pan on wire rack.

Mimi Sheraton's Double Chocolate Pudding

Most of us are rightly satisfied when it comes to such store-bought staples as potato chips and chocolate pudding. They're available in convenient packages, they require little preparation, and they taste good, so who ever thinks of making them from scratch?

My friend Mimi Sheraton does, and this double chocolate pudding is just one of her homemade originals. Try it and I think you'll agree there are times when convenience is worth sacrificing.

Makes 4 large or 6 small servings

2 squares unsweetened chocolate
1 cup, minus 2 tablespoons sugar
2 cups milk
⅛ teaspoon salt
3 tablespoons cornstarch
3 tablespoons unsweetened cocoa powder (not a mix)
2 tablespoons cold, unsalted butter (see note)
½ teaspoon vanilla

1. Chop or grate the chocolate squares; place in top of a double boiler over gently boiling water. (The water should just barely touch the bottom of the upper pot.)

2. Stir in sugar, 1⅔ cups milk, and salt. Heat, stirring constantly, until chocolate melts and mixture is well blended.

3. While chocolate melts, sift cornstarch and cocoa powder together onto wax paper; stir into ⅓ cup milk in a cup.

4. Stir cornstarch mixture into chocolate; continue cooking and stirring gently for 7 to 8 minutes, or until pudding thickens and almost mounds.

5. Cover and cook, without stirring, for 10 minutes. Remove top of double boiler from water; gently stir in butter, cut into tiny pieces. Cool 5 to 7 minutes, then stir in vanilla. Pour into individual dessert dishes or a serving bowl; cover with wax paper to prevent a skin from forming. Cool, then chill a few hours. Serve with a topping of whipped cream, if you wish.

Note: Omit salt from ingredients if salted butter is used.

Nika Hazelton's Rødgrød

Rødgrød, or red pudding, is to the Danes what apple pie is to Americans—a popular classic that's easy to make and most enjoyable to sample. This is Nika Hazelton's version (everyone in Denmark has his own), and it's particularly good when made with fresh fruits. But frozen ones will do nicely and, for the sake of convenience, this is what Nika calls for in the ingredients list. Served with slivered almonds and heavy cream, rødgrød may convert even staunch apple-pie fans. At any rate, you'll find it tempting.

Makes 6 servings

---

2 packages (10 ounces each) frozen raspberries, thawed
2 packages (10 ounces each) frozen strawberries, thawed
⅓ cup cornstarch
½ cup water
1 tablespoon lemon juice
    Sugar
⅓ cup blanched, slivered almonds (optional)
    Heavy cream, unbeaten

1. Combine berries and their syrups in a saucepan. Bring to the boiling point, stirring occasionally. Press mixture through a fine sieve; return to pan.

2. Mix cornstarch with water to form a smooth paste.
3. Bring fruit back to the boiling point; lower heat and stir in cornstarch mixture. Cook, stirring constantly, for about 3 minutes, or until mixture becomes completely transparent. Remove from heat; stir in lemon juice.
4. Pour fruit into a glass serving dish and sprinkle top with a little sugar; cool. Cover and chill for 2 hours or overnight. Before serving, decorate with the almonds. Serve with heavy cream.

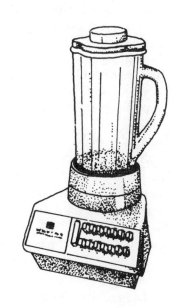

Fauchon's Chocolate Mousse

The next time you're in Paris head for Fauchon's on the Rue Madeleine. This elegant gourmet shop is one place you'll remember long after your passport expires. The desserts are, in a word, terrific. Thanks to the efforts of a roving editor for Family Circle, *and to the generosity of Fauchon's director, I have this chocolate mousse recipe for you.*

Makes 10 servings

3 squares unsweetened chocolate
2 ounces sweet cooking chocolate
5 egg yolks
¾ cup sugar
½ teaspoon vanilla
4 egg whites
1¼ cups heavy cream, stiffly beaten

1. Melt chocolate in top of a double boiler over hot, not boiling water. Remove top of double boiler from water; cool.
2. Beat egg yolks with ½ cup sugar in a medium-size bowl until light and thick; beat in cooled chocolate mixture. Stir in vanilla.
3. Beat egg whites in large bowl of electric mixer until foamy-white and double in volume. Add remaining ¼ cup sugar slowly, 1 tablespoon at a time, beating until meringue stands in firm peaks.
4. Beat about ¼ cup of the meringue into chocolate mixture. Fold in beaten cream and remaining meringue until no streaks of white remain. Reserve 1½ cups of mixture and refrigerate until serving time. Spoon remaining mousse into an 8-cup serving dish. Refrigerate at least 2 hours.
5. Before serving, carefully pipe the reserved mousse mixture through a pastry bag fitted with a large notched tip, in swirls for a decorative top.

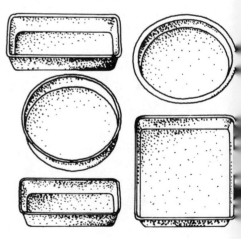

Ann Seranne's Foolproof Crème Brûlée

Crème brûlée or, in the English vernacular, custard pudding with a broiled brown-sugar topping, is one dessert I particularly enjoy after a heavy meal—it slides down so easily. But making it can be another matter entirely. With some recipes, the cream curdles or the brown sugar burns. I mentioned this to Ann Seranne recently, and she volunteered this recipe, along with some good advice.

"Use an ample-sized, very heavy, cast aluminum saucepan," Ann suggests, "and it will be difficult to curdle the cream. Also, when you run the sugar-covered pudding under the broiler, keep your eye on it." She elaborates by giving specific timing directions in the recipe. All in all, I think you'll find the recipe not only "foolproof," but good—sinfully good, in fact.

Makes 4 to 6 servings

7 large egg yolks
4 tablespoons sugar
1 tablespoon cornstarch
3 cups heavy cream
1 tablespoon vanilla
1 cup firmly packed light brown sugar

1. Combine egg yolks, sugar, and cornstarch in a large bowl. Beat with mixer at high speed until mixture is thick and pale in color, 2 to 3 minutes.
2. Heat cream to very hot or just simmering around the edges in a heavy, 6- to 8-cup, cast aluminum saucepan. Gradually pour hot cream into egg yolk mixture, beating constantly. (The mixture should be like a thick custard at this point.)
3. Pour egg yolk-cream mixture back into the hot saucepan and cook over medium heat, stirring rapidly and constantly with a wooden spoon (making sure you reach all over bottom and sides of the pan). Watch carefully. As soon as the cream rises and foams up in the pan and begins to simmer around the edges, remove from heat but continue to stir rapidly for 1 or 2 minutes. It will not be quite thick enough, so return to heat and stir rapidly until it rises up once again in the pan. Again remove from heat and continue to stir rapidly until cream is very thick. Immediately place pan into a shallow pan of cold water to stop further cooking; stir in vanilla.
4. Pour into a crystal or china bowl and refrigerate overnight.

5. The next day, wrap dish in heavy aluminum foil to protect it from the broiler heat. Sprinkle brown sugar evenly over top. Broil 3 inches from source of heat for 4 to 5 minutes, until sugar carmelizes. Watch carefully for it is very easy to burn the sugar. Chill again until ready to serve.

The Best-Ever Chocolate Chip Cookies

Chocolate chip cookies are not really a dessert. They're something I can handle before, after, or between meals, and this is my favorite recipe for them. Unlike some, this recipe has enough "chips" to do the name proud.

Makes 3½ dozen cookies

1¾ cups sifted all-purpose flour
½ teaspoon baking soda
¼ teaspoon salt
12 tablespoons (1½ sticks) butter
½ cup granulated sugar
¼ cup firmly packed brown sugar
1 egg
1 teaspoon vanilla
1 cup chopped walnuts
1 6-ounce package semisweet chocolate pieces

1. Measure flour, baking soda, and salt onto a piece of wax paper.
2. Beat butter, granulated sugar, brown sugar, egg, and vanilla in a large bowl, until fluffy.
3. Add flour mixture, stirring until well blended. Stir in nuts and chocolate pieces.
4. Drop by rounded teaspoonfuls, 1 inch apart, onto greased cooky sheets.
5. Bake in a moderate oven, 350 degrees, for 8 minutes, or until golden brown. Remove from cooky sheets; cool on wire racks.

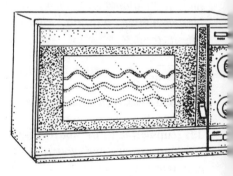

My Mother's Mocha Nut Butter Cookies

My mother is a really good cook— but then I don't know anyone who doesn't enjoy his own mother's cooking. Anyway, she is good and, like many women who also enjoy cooking, she is always ready to try new recipes, particularly ones her friends recommend. This recipe, for instance, is one she borrowed from Mrs. Helen Kirkpatrick, a friend in Floral Park, New York. It has become, by popular family demand, part of my mother's own recipe collection, and I've included it here so that you may borrow it, too.

Makes about 3 dozen cookies

½ pound (2 sticks) butter, softened
½ cup granulated sugar
1¾ cups all-purpose flour
¼ cup unsweetened cocoa
2 teaspoons vanilla
2 teaspoons instant coffee
½ teaspoon salt
2 cups finely chopped nuts
    Confectioners sugar

1. Cream butter and granulated sugar in a large bowl until light and fluffy.
2. Add flour, cocoa, vanilla, coffee, salt, and nuts; mix until well blended.
3. Shape dough into 1-inch balls and place, about 1 inch apart, on buttered cookie sheets.
4. Bake in a moderate oven, 325 degrees, for about 15 minutes. Cool on wire racks. Roll in confectioners sugar and store in an airtight container.

Emily's Walnut Crescents

Peg Bracken is a good judge of food and when she said these are "approximately the greatest cookies," I took her word for it. She got the recipe from someone named Emily, thus the title. True to her word, the cookies turned out to be delicious creations.

Makes about 4 dozen

  1 **cup walnuts, pounded or ground to a paste (use the blender)**
½ **pound (2 sticks) butter, softened**
½ **teaspoon vanilla**
¾ **cup granulated sugar**
2½ **cups sifted flour**
  1 **cup confectioners sugar**

1. Mix walnuts, butter, vanilla, granulated sugar, and flour together in a large bowl. Shape dough into small lozenges or small crescents. Place on an ungreased cookie sheet.
2. Bake in a moderate oven, 350 degrees, for 15 minutes. While the first batch bakes, sift the confectioners sugar and have it ready to dip the cookies in after they've cooled for a minute or so.

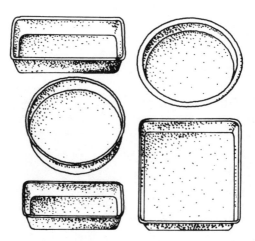

Index